"Mark Graham has writt[en]
the Harassment of Hum[an Fears]
to battle irrational fears. This book [is a]
treatment. It is all about Christ and the glory of God. For those Chris[tians]
who are willing to work on Pastor Graham's suggestions, meditate on
the many Scriptures that he recommends, and seek God with a heart of
faith, there is amazing hope that God will renew their mind and relieve
them of their fears. Pastor Graham knows what he is talking about as
he chronicles his own journey of panic and fear. This is a book to read
carefully, pondering each and every Scripture that is included. I am glad
that I had the opportunity to read it, and I highly recommend it to you.

-Martha Peace, biblical counselor and author of *The Excellent Wife*

"This book is a unique blend of theological truths, practical illustrations,
and counseling insights designed to equip the reader in his or her battle
with anxiety. The author's own struggles shared transparently make this
book a must-read for anyone who has dealt with the disabling effects of
fear and longs for effective strategies. Scripture-saturated, Christ-centered,
and hope-stirring—"Harnessing the Harassment of Human Fears" arms
and inspires the reader to realize freedom from crippling fear!"

—Mrs. Julie Lewis, M.A. Ed, a pastor's wife and
Dean of English at Antietam Bible College

"If you want a devastating blow to your crippling fears, then read this book
slowly and seriously. Mercilessly apply the biblical practicum against the
foreboding phobias of the flesh and I am certain you will begin to taste the
sweet victory of calm and confidence in Christ!"

—Pastor Nathaniel Graham, Berean Community
Bible Church, Milford, Delaware.

Harnessing the Harassment of Human Fears

Tactical Tales/Timeless Truths

MARK L. GRAHAM

CROSSBOOKS
PUBLISHING

CrossBooks™
A Division of LifeWay
1663 Liberty Drive
Bloomington, IN 47403
www.crossbooks.com
Phone: 1-866-879-0502

© 2013 Mark L. Graham. All rights reserved.

No part of this book may be reproduced, stored in a retrieval system, or transmitted by any means without the written permission of the author.

First published by CrossBooks 10/24/2013

ISBN: 978-1-4627-3218-0 (sc)
ISBN: 978-1-4627-3219-7 (hc)
ISBN: 978-1-4627-3220-3 (e)

Library of Congress Control Number: 2013918263

Printed in the United States of America.

This book is printed on acid-free paper.

Any people depicted in stock imagery provided by Thinkstock are models, and such images are being used for illustrative purposes only. Certain stock imagery © Thinkstock.

Scripture taken from the New King James Version. Copyright 1979, 1980, 1982 by Thomas Nelson, inc. Used by permission. All rights reserved.

Because of the dynamic nature of the Internet, any web addresses or links contained in this book may have changed since publication and may no longer be valid. The views expressed in this work are solely those of the author and do not necessarily reflect the views of the publisher, and the publisher hereby disclaims any responsibility for them.

Acknowledgments

First and above all else, I am indebted to Jesus Christ, who is gracious to impart wisdom upon whom He wills for whatever function or role He deems necessary to accomplish His own glory. My high school counselor questioned my college aspirations. He had the data and concluded that I "was not college material," but off I went to college on academic probation. Christ saw beyond appearance and effectually ministered to my need. It was not so much the potential He saw in me but the investment of Himself that He chose to make in an unlikely life that was a little rough around the edges. I am forever complete in the life that I enjoy through grace, alone.

Thanks to my beloved wife who has been my primary counselor throughout my pastoral labors. Diane has given me strength for my weaknesses, encouragement in my despair, and joy in our pilgrimage together. She has fulfilled so many labors of love that her example to her family and many others is honored and well known. Thank you, my love, for the countless hours you have spent to bring about a sensible read.

I thank my eldest daughter, Julie, who amid her busy schedule as a mother, pastor's wife, and professor has made it a priority to peruse her dad's writing project.

Thank you to my son, Nate, who helped me by answering several technical questions out of the original language, as well as by ongoing incentives to labor on and finish well.

I am grateful also to my son-in-law, Chris Fisher, who has pledged his help and expertise in giving this volume public visibility through a variety of media means.

A special thanks to Jeff Lyons, who provided on-call technical support and always with a joyful spirit.

The Grace Bible Church deserves acknowledgment for their devotion of prayer, encouragement, and helpful feedback through the composition of this book. I am sincerely thankful to a church fellowship that enables her pastor to minister "with joy and not with grief."

My sincere appreciation to Crossbooks for a very helpful and positive experience in publishing my writing project through them. Thank you.

Finally, this book is a tribute to my children and their spouses, all of whom love Christ and endeavor to serve Him faithfully through their churches and various ministries: daughter Julie Lewes and her husband, Pastor Conroy; daughter Jennifer Fisher and her husband, Christopher; son, Pastor Nate, and his wife, Kimberly; daughter Kristen and her husband, Scott.

I thank God for blessing my wife, Diane, and me with such a family who continually strengthen our every effort in the gospel. I trust this book will be useful to their lives and service in the gospel.

Dedication

To my dearest Friend
and to all those precious gifts of grace
that He has granted me in a
loving wife and serving children.
To all my teachers
of the past and present.

Table of Contents

Foreword by Mark Ransom xi
Introduction xv

CHAPTER 1
Encounters, Episodes, and the Experiences of Fear 1

CHAPTER 2
Fictitious Myths and a Familiar Case 7

CHAPTER 3
Contacts, Connections, and Counsel 19

CHAPTER 4
Matters of Management and Mastery 31

CHAPTER 5
Sticks, Slingshots, and Other Proven Methods 49

CHAPTER 6
Lateral Help for Languishing Hearts 75

CHAPTER 7
Practicum 107

A Concluding Q and A Session 133
Some Enduring Resources 141

FOREWORD
by Mark Ransom

When my friend, Dr. Mark Graham, called me and asked if I would write the Foreword to this book, *Harnessing the Harassment of Human Fears*, I was not immediately thrilled with the idea. Looking back on that phone call, I remember three things happening.

First, the momentary silence of disbelief, *Is he really serious? I can't believe he is asking this of me.*

Second, as my friend continued to explain his request I thought, *there is no way I can do this*. I am not eloquent of speech (verbal or written); *I am simply a pastor of a country church in a town of which few have heard; besides, what will he or others think of me when they read it* (sound like fear?).

Third, once I walked back into the conscience presence of my Savior and Master, I said to my friend, "I am humbled and honored that you have asked me—yes, I will write it."

I was brought to faith in Christ as my Savior at age thirteen in 1967 at the Word of Life Ranch in Schroon Lake, NY. It wasn't until my early twenties that I came to understand God's calling to pastoral ministry. After receiving my Bible college education at Calvary Bible College, Kansas City, Missouri, and then getting most of the way through seminary at Baptist Bible Seminary, Clarks Summit, PA, I began pastoring a church in rural, upstate NY in 1997. Four years later, the Lord led us to our present ministry just north of Syracuse, NY in another rural setting of Constantia Center.

About a year into this ministry, the Lord brought Dr. Mark Graham into my life. As I was going through my mail one day, I came across an invitation from him (it was actually addressed to the previous pastor). As I read the invitation, my heart jumped; *I need this* (I had come to Constantia Center with baggage)! So I called Dr. Graham and signed onto his mentoring and accountability group for men. The Lord graciously brought joy and freedom in my life through the counsel of this humble, generous, skillful, and Christ exalting counselor as he effectively used the powerful and sufficient Word of God.

Since that time, Pastor Graham has been a valued mentor, fellow pastor and counselor, and dear friend. That same humble, skillful and Christ-exalting counsel that I found in Dr. Graham in that accountability group is also found in the pages of this book that you hold in your hands.

This book is for the child of God who desires to live in the joy and freedom that Jesus purchased for His people on Calvary. Jesus died for our joy—the joy of knowing, loving, and serving God in a large place, not in a strait place dominated by the bondage of fear.

With laser-like precision and God given wisdom, Dr. Graham accurately exposits the reality of irrational fear that nips at the heels of many followers of Jesus (and for some, downright incapacitates).

Through biblical truth and reasoning he brings the fear struggler *into* battle against this very real adversary, not away from the battle; he brings him into the circle with God, his strong and mighty Redeemer.

With insight, compassion, and clarity, Mark Graham helps the reader grapple with the issue of avoiding or denying irrational fear through medication as he clearly and accurately states the Bible's view of struggle: there is value in the struggle because that is where faith is stretched and strengthened, where joy and peace are had, where God is glorified as His child trusts/rests in Him and obeys His Word.

This is not a "let go and let God" treatise, rather it is a practical,

Christ-centered how-to manual for the Christian who understands that God intends His redeemed child to be actively involved in the putting off of the old and the putting on of the new in Jesus Christ.

Dr. Graham does not deal with this subject of irrational fear from a detached clinician's point of view; rather he puts himself right out there as he relays his own personal battles against ungodly fear—as a wrestler, father, pastor/teacher, and medical patient.

So the insights found in this book have been incubated over time in the hothouse of the life of a redeemed man doing battle against the irrational fears of his unredeemed humanness, for God's glory and for his joy in Christ.

This book bleeds Bible; it is readable and understandable by both counselor and counselee. It is good medicine for the one who struggles with irrational fear and for those helping others in this battle. It has ministered to me in my fears. Thank you, my friend, for getting in the circle with God and teaching us to do the same.

To God be the glory!

Mark Ransom
Pastor
Constantia Center Baptist Church
Constantia, NY

Introduction

Helping those who fear is certainly intended with the writing of this book. It is not, however, the primary goal. If, by this text, I am used to advance any struggling heart to draw closer to wisdom at its very source, then the project has been a success. The Bible God is surely my inference as the source of all wisdom, but what *is* wisdom that it should be the goal of this book, yea, the goal of our lives? "Wisdom in Scripture," says R. C. Sproul, "means choosing the best and noblest end at which to aim, along with the most appropriate and effective means of achieving that end."[1] There are, thus, many things we could suggest as helps, remedies, and counsel, which might seem pertinent to our discussion of irrational fears, but there is no help, remedy, or counsel so noble, so fulfilling, so meaningful, so fruitful and deeply healing as the wisdom that comes from Jesus Christ (Col 2:3). In fact, Christian wisdom is said to be the fear of God (Prov. 1:7; 9:10; Eccl. 12:13), and it is in the fear of God where the truest antidote for irrational fear is found. In my lifelong struggle with various fears, I have found great hope, comfort, and, above all else, peace of mind in the pursuit of godly wisdom. Dealing with irrational fears may be perceived as nonsensical battles with insanity fought in the sterile vacuum of mere human effort; God's wisdom, however, restores purpose, perspective, and power to manage conflict in such a way that He is glorified as the end result.

So this book is offered up to God to help the fearful know His wisdom in a genuine and practical way. The reading at hand is intended not to be exhaustive but as a building block upon which the reader can discover for himself, or herself a plethora of gold out of the treasury of God's wisdom. Truly, "He does great things past finding out. Yes, wonders without number" (Job 9:10). The wisdom of God has enabled me to see irrational fear as my opportunity to:

- understand my weaknesses and vulnerabilities and the sufficiency of God's promise to endure the obstacles to faith;
- discover more deeply my own creaturehood and my desperate need to rely heavily upon God's utter sovereignty; and
- experience more fully the reality of faith that belongs to those who are serious about traveling the road of conformity to the image of God's Son.

Irrational fears become sort of an ally to grace, odd in the sense that fears would not appear to be up to any good in our lives were it not for God's promise that "all things work together for good to those who love God, to those who are the called according to His purpose" (Rom 8:28). The "called" are summoned of God to a pathway of purpose where the soul is tried at every turn while the heart of the elect son clings fast to the love that will never let go, not in this life nor the life to come. Odd, too, is the notion that I would rather forgo the opportunity of fear—that is, I would welcome the refining benefit of struggle—but my flesh still abhors the feel, the agony, the suffering. If I could possibly avoid the battle, I would; but I cannot escape the fray in good conscience, so I will persevere to be battle ready. This is my lot, my appointment of grace, and this is the way of spiritual growth and maturity until the glorious liberty of the children of God (Rom 8:21).

The outlay of the book is forthright and self-evident, with a good deal of practical helps in the final chapter. The helps are samplings to incite exercise and expertise in the skill of fending off panic. The illustrations throughout are given to identify with the reader's own experience of fear by providing a window to view the author's fraternal conflict.

May God grant insight, strength, and courage to Christians everywhere by the hope offered within these pages. May God grant sight through the presentation of the glorious gospel of Jesus Christ to all those who may have come upon this book accidently on purpose.

Mark L. Graham

"For God has not given us a spirit of fearfulness, but one of power, love, and sound judgment."

2 Timothy 1:7
The Apologetics Study Bible (Nashville, TN: Holman Bible Publishers, 2007)

CHAPTER 1

Encounters, Episodes, and the Experiences of Fear

So there we were. My sixteen-year-old son, Nathaniel, greeted me at mat side where I had just emerged unscored upon in tournament competition and champion of the Watkins Glen Wrestling Festival at the ripe old age of forty-four! "Go for it, Dad," my son said. "Enter another tournament!" But I reminded him of the difference between us: "When you finish a wrestling match," I told him, "you're looking for oranges, but when the buzzer ends my bout, I'm looking for oxygen!"

In reflection, wrestling has played a big part in my life. From fulfilling a boyhood dream by making the high school varsity team to winning a national collegiate title, the sport ran through my blood; it drew out my deepest emotions—but also my deepest fears. You see, the truth is, this athlete struggled with claustrophobia, and behind every opponent was the ominous fear of being held down, pinned down, or tied up. It was a secret: a personal battle that I endured throughout the eight years of my wrestling career. It seemed the culprit of several defeats and, at times, the reason for advantage as I scrambled frantically to get loose. Truly, this raw fear was the greatest challenge of my sports experience! Fear was the unwelcome phantom.

Make no mistake about it, the experience of fear is real; the encounter is unnerving and traumatic. The episode is, from all appearances, unlike any other form of suffering. The phobic reaction is like an invisible force that grips the heart of human feeling and sense, leaving the sufferer stripped, defeated, washed up, and wrung out. The crude and cruel aspect of one's battle with fear is the haunting awareness that this opponent is ever stalking, always lurking, unrelenting, and overpowering. Like a personal tour of the gas ovens of Auschwitz, a visible reflection of the fearful episode indelibly etches the horror into one's mind, making recovery, at least from the sufferer's angle, a virtual impossibility. To this belief, most sufferers will readily admit.

In my experience helping those who fear, the stimulus of fear is multidirectional, sometimes complex and hard to figure—making the fear episode feel unique and impossible to overcome. As we will discuss later, these fearful experiences are amazingly similar at their core, symptomatically calculated, and generally in concert with what we might expect from a fear episode (1 Cor 10:13).[1] The triggers, however, may be radically diverse and multidirectional. As there is but one true sense behind any biblical narrative (2 Tim 2:15),[2] so fear is the unmistakable force behind a plethora of stimuli from the context of life.

The following list is a brief overview of irrational fears, along with their categorical identity/stimulus.

1. Acrophobia: fear of high places
2. Agoraphobia: fear of large or open places
3. Algophobia: fear of pain or discomfort
4. Astraphobia: fear of severe weather
5. Claustrophobia: fear of close or closed places
6. Hematophobia: fear of blood (the thought of blood)
7. Mysophobia: fear of germs
8. Monophobia: fear of being alone, without other people
9. Nyctophobia: fear of darkness
10. Ocholophobia: fear of crowds
11. Pathophobia: fear of disease
12. Pyrophobia: fear of fire
13. Zoophobia: fear of animals

Diagram 1
The Fearful Episode and Effect

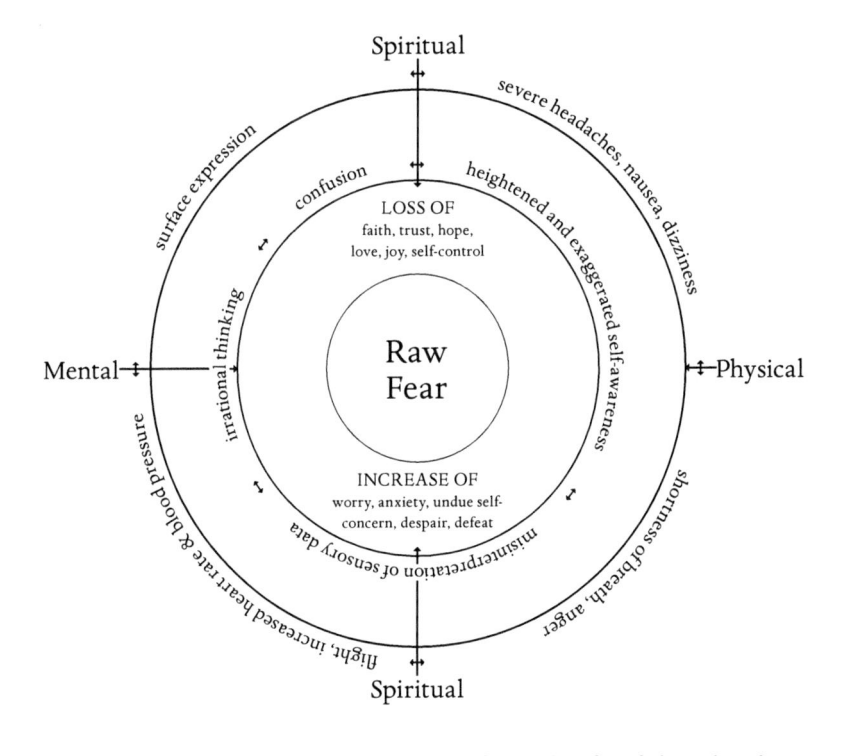

Spiritual

- severe headaches, nausea, dizziness
- heightened and exaggerated self-awareness
- misinterpretation of sensory data
- flight, increased heart rate and blood pressure
- shortness of breath, anger
- irrational thinking
- surface expression
- confusion

LOSS OF faith, trust, hope, love, joy, self-control

Raw Fear

INCREASE OF worry, anxiety, undue self-concern, despair, defeat

Mental — Physical

Spiritual

Like a balloon, the fear episode is inflated by fearful, redundant reasoning. As the triggers incite feelings of helplessness and panic, the painful experience is heightened. Remember that the stimuli is diverse and shows up on life's doorstep whenever and however; but, bottom line, fearful, cyclic thinking pumps energy into irrational fears. Truly, and in the words of Franklin D. Roosevelt, "We have nothing to fear but fear itself."[3] In our case, the issue that must ultimately be addressed is the "fear" and the way we think about fear, for the stimulus is never the fundamental issue; the stimulus is simply life.

3

Few of us who know fear battle with only one trigger, one stimulus. Most of us who know fear battle with a diversity of stimuli.

My pastoral ministry has spanned nearly forty years, during which time I've also taught biblical counseling at the seminary level and directed the Genesis Counseling Services. Obviously, my labors took me to church pulpits, school chapels, and numerous radio opportunities. I've also enjoyed a limited number of conference engagements, addressing both pastors and parishioners. God's calling on my life and my serving Him in this capacity has been the ambition of my heart since coming to Jesus at the young age of nine.

There is nothing else in life for which I am better suited than serving the Lord as a shepherd, yet there have been few challenges in life that I have found more difficult than public speaking. Yes, you've probably guessed it. I have encountered the fear of stage fright.

Although I cannot recollect my original conflict, I do recall an increasing struggle when speaking from my regular church pulpit sometime after the first ten years of pastoral ministry. I remember losing my place often in the sermon presentation. My thoughts seemed scattered as I typically honed in on what part of my message might "throw me" or send me into a full-blown fear episode (where my mouth became dry and my verbiage more breathy). I was keenly aware of blushing and of how people might perceive me at that moment.

Interestingly, those who know me best, my wife and family, observed only slight indications that I was emotionally "off course." However, the fear experience became so intense in my head that I came to a place where leaving the ministry was a very real consideration. You see, though my raging battle was hardly recognizable to others, it meant a continued agony for me and something I honestly felt I could not handle without eventual emotional breakdown or heart failure.

Of all the thoughts rushing through my head, the most prominent was preoccupation! The fear of my fears seemed inescapable, always there, night and day, occupying my tomorrows and whatever my speaking assignment might entail; public prayer, small or larger group devotionals, Bible studies, funerals, weddings, class settings, pulpit ministry, interviews, etc. Any situation in which I opened my mouth in the presence of others could incite an episode so discomfiting that I thought to run, to hide, to avoid, to quit! Truly, I was dreading life more with every passing day.

Now, I share these things for no other motivation than to come alongside those who have mutually suffered and to provide viable assistance. The reader who has known the heartache that fear brings will identify with the pain of a common human experience. The reader will also peer between the lines and envision the context of the dreaded adversary we call fear. Here, the embattled must not reside, remain, or root. Even identity, mutual experience, and commonalities may adversely affect the fearing heart if one chooses to focus on the episode as an end in itself. Searching for the perfect depiction of one's dilemma, hunting for one's diagnostic label, or developing a network of victims anonymous may do nothing more than consensually reinforce the stimuli for fear—heightening the episode.

Helping those who fear is the intention of this manual. The question that must be asked at this juncture is the one Jesus asked an afflicted man many years ago: "Do you want to be healed?" (Jn 5:6).[4] And what kind of question is that, after all? What sufferer wouldn't want the obvious? Yet it is a plausible question because the motivations of our hearts can be, so often, the real culprits of our infirmity. What we need is not always what we desire, and what we need for our help is not always the avenue we are willing to walk. Looking back, I rejoice at where I have come in the management of fear, but the help Jesus prescribes is not the pathway I would have chosen, in and of myself. Stay with me!

Chapter One Endnotes

[1] *The Reformation Study Bible.* general editor R.C. Sproul (Lake Mary, FL: Ligonier Ministries, 2005), 1214.

[2] First Corinthians 10:13. I have cited this reference to demonstrate the biblicality of the thinking that suggests that human beings share a commonality in their struggles. As we will see in the further study of this verse, the fear episode fits well within the range of application here.

[3] Second Timothy 2:15. This text teaches there is but one true sense to any given passage of Scripture. The Greek language for *rightly dividing* (NKJV) may also be rendered, *straightly cutting.* There is one true interpretation to Holy Scripture, although there may be multiple applications.

[4] *The Public Papers of F.D.R., Vol. 2: The Year of Crisis, 1933.* Editor, Samuel Rosenman (NY: Random House, 1938).

[5] John 5:6. "Do you want to be made well?" (NKJV). The Bible tells us that Jesus knew, in Himself, that the man who lay by the Bethesda Pool had been infirmed a "long time," in fact, for "thirty-eight years" (5:5). Knowing the situation of the man, the Messiah would well know exactly what the sufferer wanted. The question of the Lord begs a faith response.

CHAPTER 2

Fictitious Myths and a Familiar Case

In an attempt to better evaluate the nature of fear and understand further the fixation that seems to trouble our sanity, I will offer some strategic finds and observations. Think of our present discussion as fundamental insight or essential data that will enable us to dispel certain myths or fallacies that often surround the fear experience.

About Myths and Fallacies

Very probably, the greatest myth of the fear encounter rests with the lie of our mind that says, *I can't do this!* It may be public speaking or simply opening your home to your neighbors for an evening of hospitality. It may be something quite different, such as driving over a bridge or through the Lincoln Tunnel. Possibly, it is the fear of ever being alone, or just the opposite—the fear of being in a group or crowd of people. But whatever the stimulus, the lie is the same: *I can't do this!* And, herein, is the beginning of defeat and the slippery slope of our undoing. Clearly, this is a lie, an untruth set off in our heads. Underscore this reality and mark it well: it is simply not true that I can't do this! The phrase is nothing more than a self-fulfilling prophecy. If it is true, it is because we make it so and for no other reason. Bottom line, the fearful person recounts an earlier fearful experience or gives thought to former episodes and hoists the flag of surrender, making the choice to succumb to the path of least resistance (or so he thinks). Everyone gets weary in warfare. No one enjoys a perpetual career in hand-to-hand combat. "Ah gets weary an' tired of tryin'," is the best analysis of what happens at ground zero in the fear experience. We just don't want the hassle anymore; therefore, *I refuse. I won't. I can't.*

Somewhere in my harried entanglement with stage fright, I was invited to the chapel service of a respected Bible college in southern New York. I was to address the student body and faculty for better than forty minutes on a very "special day." Now, the particulars as to what that "special day" involved only came to me after the chapel service (thank the Lord!). I accepted the engagement out of sheer obedience to Christ. After all, I was a servant of God.

The president of the college had personally asked me to come. It was my opportunity to make an impact upon an upcoming generation of pastors, missionaries, and Christian leaders. Declining the invitation was not an option for me; thus, I said yes to Jesus Christ, while my flesh kicked and screamed. Quite honestly, I went to that college pulpit with a contrite spirit, a heart bowed in utter dependence on Christ—I had no haughty look of vanity; I was just emptied and bankrupt.

God had this servant exactly where He wanted him—speaking to the deeper need of the student, faculty, and, yes, a visiting academic accrediting body whom the Lord had summoned for reasons of "higher learning." I don't know what God had in mind for those to whom I ministered that day; that was His business and mine was to follow Him straight through the sensation of my deepest dread.

Did I relish the experience of inner agony? No! And, no, I don't want to go that way again, but if God asks me to get out of the boat into the howling storm, I will, for "I can do all things through Christ who strengthens me" (Phlp 4:13).[1]

Am I to tell you that Jesus took away the dark swells, boisterous winds, and suffocating waters—those noisy elements of my heart and flesh? Can't say He took them all away, my friend, and I'm not convinced He promises an escape route that doesn't try the soul. It's just that I am learning to see the fallacies of my fears and the lies in my head. *I can't* is a myth if I am truly a child of God. Grace will see me through, and I will always look back from a pleasant hilltop.

This I do know to be true: any lie that prevents obedience to the expressed will of God is neither sensible nor sane. For those who have chosen to walk on in their trouble, denying fear's big myth, progress of faith has resulted. This progress of faith (observed both in myself and those under my care) is likewise multidirectional and broadening to one's experience of hope (Rom. 5:3, 4).[2] In reality, the tribulation of fear will strip its subject of all self-possession when Christ is wholly followed. This is a good thing. This is personally liberating.

A further fallacy of the fear episode is the belief that giving in or giving up will bring me relief. It is the pathway of least resistance. Be it *I refuse, I won't, I can't* or the route of high-tailed avoidance, these non confrontational approaches actually validate the myth of fear's omnipotence in our minds. Avoidance gives false credibility to a lie. Surrendering to fear's intimidation solidifies the deluded belief that *I can't*. Hiding or running away adds to the twisted notion that, given time, my fears will dissipate or at least decrease. Abnormal fears do not disappear by avoidance. The tendency of irrational fears is to hunt you down, find you out, and box you in! Life cannot be sidestepped. It just has a way of showing up on our doorstep!

A Familiar Case

Once again, the real truth of the matter is this: any headway, recovery, or relief we might gain in this conflict will come only as we square off with the challenge.

Diagram 2
The Faith Episode and Effect

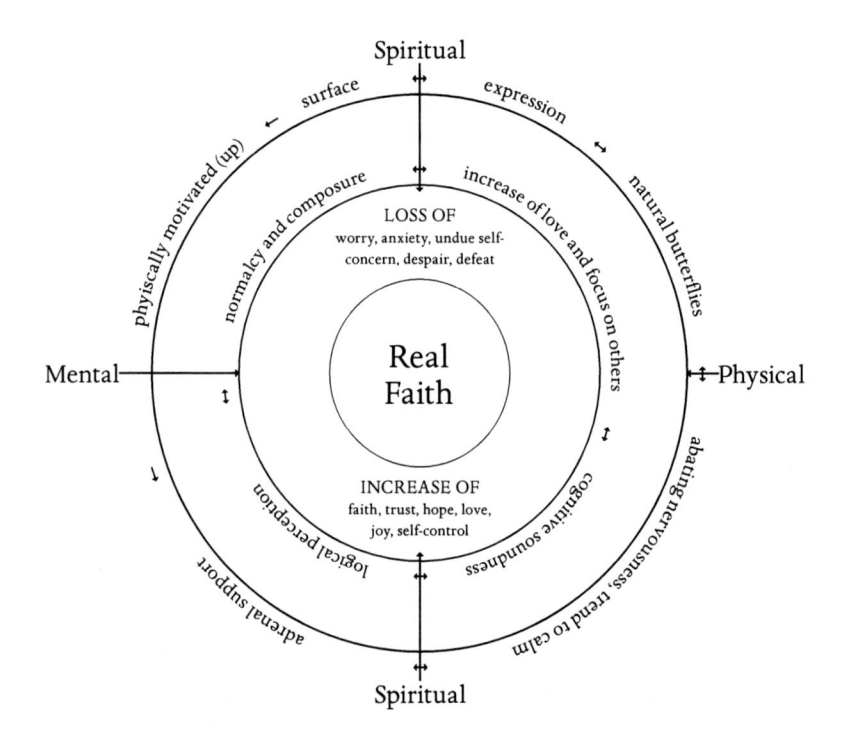

Outer ring (Spiritual — top, Spiritual — bottom; Mental — left, Physical — right):
- surface
- expression
- physically motivated (up)
- natural butterflies
- normalcy and composure
- increase of love and focus on others
- logical perception
- cognitive soundness
- adrenal support
- abating nervousness, trend to calm

Inner ring:
- LOSS OF worry, anxiety, undue self-concern, despair, defeat
- INCREASE OF faith, trust, hope, love, joy, self-control

Center: Real Faith

Likewise, the faith episode is strengthened by the continued posturing of biblical reasoning. The triggers are met with the force of objective truth, and healing for mind and body ensue. Thus, when life shows up, whenever and however, a habit of sound thinking corrals the stampede of irrational fear.

HARNESSING THE HARASSMENT OF HUMAN FEARS

I am reminded of Israel's encounter with the Philistine warrior named Goliath of Gath. Let's look at the situation of David and Goliath again from the sidelines. Let's sit together as close as we can to the event. We're looking for data relative to our discussion of fear, of faith. We simply do not want to miss the details of a "good fight" (1 Sam 17).³

Well, Goliath is formidable enough! Our passage tells several things about him. Generally, we understand a cubit to be approximately eighteen inches. There is some discussion that the cubit, here, might have been twenty-one inches, which would put this warrior above eleven feet tall. Using the commonly accepted standard of eighteen inches, Goliath was undoubtedly the largest man known in history, measuring nine feet tall. This opponent was not the gangly sort. Goliath of Gath, whose name might indicate that he was quite possibly a mercenary and not a Philistine by blood, was a huge man, a giant of a man—a man whose frame was large enough to manage his weight of armor with agility.

- A helmet of bronze: The actual weight of the helmet is unknown, but it would have been forged with the dual purpose of protection and intimidation. It was naturally the first thing noticed. It was stimulus for fear (v. 5).

- A coat of mail: This protective body cover alone weighed 125 pounds or "five thousand shekels of bronze" (v. 5). Have you ever tried to manage two packages of roofing shingles on your shoulders at once, or a 100-pound bag of cement? The man was a monster!

- A bronze javelin [affixed] between his shoulders: The javelin was polished to be seen and well-balanced to be thrown for an Olympian toss. Goliath was very good at the javelin throw, evidently the best. He was a champion (v. 6).

- The spear: Oh, yes, the spear of this talented warrior was a staff "like a weaver's beam." The best analogy for us would be throwing a fence post made of ironwood or locust (v. 7).

- His iron spearhead: You didn't think we were finished with our description, did you? Our fearful adversary has a spear with an iron head weighing fifteen pounds or "six hundred shekels." What you've got is a powerful, spring-loaded ramming iron. Such a weapon thrust from such a large man would normally have its effect on several men who might lunge forth in formation (v. 7).

- A shield bearer went before him: a hand-picked young man, who would, himself, appear strong and hostile. A man, bearing a shield, who announced Goliath's presence and introduced his dread. Just imagine it! Just let your mind wander ... (v. 7).

- Goliath's sword: We didn't catch this weapon in our immediate text. It was there, however, since David used Goliath's own sword to kill this giant (v. 51). Possibly, the sword is not mentioned in the description of Goliath's armor because there was nothing unusual or heavy about it. You see, young David would use it momentarily, and it was light enough for David to wield it effectively. Can you contemplate the severity of a somewhat common sword in the hand of this gigantic man whose strength would count it as nothing? It would be lightning quick, shredding the flesh of anyone inside the warrior's circle.

Besides these things, the giant, Goliath, has been a man of war from his youth (v. 33). He was the reigning champ of battle-hungry warriors (v. 4). He had a loud voice and a big mouth full of profanity and curses (vv. 10, 43, 44). Lastly, Goliath had a reputation—a reputation for striking fear into the heart of his opposition. Listen carefully, now. Goliath had nurtured a habit of fear in the heart and life of every soldier belonging to Israel's host (vv. 16, 23, 24).

How was it that such a pitiful episode had gone on for so long and that all the men of Israel were dreadfully afraid? Believe me; had it not been for David's confrontation of faith, Israel would have habituated themselves to discouragement, defeat, and isolation. Wouldn't you agree that the situation from the sidelines is a bit bizarre? Intimidating, yes, but have you honestly assessed the nature of this God who fights for Israel? Have you considered His reputation from the Pentateuch, alone? Was this situation not, in the final analysis, an issue of faith for God's covenant people? Is Jehovah's help fact or fiction?

Well, we're not done here. David, a young, ruddy (British euphemism for "bloody" or healthy red), good-looking (as opposed to the leathery, scar-faced champion), baby brother sheep-keeper (vv. 42, 14, 15) was about to step up to the plate. Let's record our finds:

First: David is healthy and young; hence, he embraces the same stimuli as we all do in the face of real-life experiences:

- He *hears* Goliath's boast and defiance (v. 23).
- He *sees* Goliath's show, his pageant, and Israel's dread (vv. 24, 25)—i.e., soldiers are running scared.
- He *smells, tastes,* and *touches* the scene of battle (vv. 20–22)— i.e., shouting and fighting greets the troops.

Second: David discerned that Goliath's defiant demeanor brought reproach against Israel and against Yahweh in particular (v. 26). David assessed the event as a masquerade of fear with no rational basis for avoidance or flight. Once David had weighed the data reasonably and understood the right course of action to be taken, he was resolved to do the sane and sensible thing in the presence of his God. Any other choice than that of faith would have adverse effects, both to his personal life and upon his larger audience.

Third: David draws upon his experience of God and hastens to expend the energy of diligent faith (Heb 11:6).[4] The young steward of grace knows what must be done. He enjoins the confidence and courage of God's own Spirit and runs—that's right: David runs into the fray, assured of the outcome once he knows what is good, what is right, and what it really means to trust the living God (vv. 32–37, 40–51)! Who is boasting now? Only moments ago, Goliath would induce irrational fears. "Come to me, and I will give your flesh to the birds of the air and the beasts of the field" (v. 44). Remember that Gath's champion had even discounted David's weapon of warfare: "Am I a dog, that you come to me with sticks?" (v. 43). But who's on top now? David would not give false credibility to a lie. Faith—genuine faith, persevering faith—will not finally and ultimately surrender to intimidation, to delusion. Faith always recovers and rises to dispel myths. Faith embraces the challenge and nourishes the habit and victory of a sound mind.

It was going to be a storybook wedding. My lovely daughter, Jennifer, was about to be married. She would be the first of our four children to covenant that sacred tie. Jennifer had only recently returned from Africa, where she had taught missionary children. Now, stateside, our daughter was about to be married to a fine Christian man who would bring us three ready-made grandchildren. Our son-in-law had been a widower, and the new nanny hired on for this little tribe would become, in time, the new wife and mother. The tribe would, before very long, increase to the tune of seven children.

Oh, yes, the wedding! The promised couple was to be married in the home church where Dad would conduct the service. Family and friends would come from everywhere for God's storybook wedding. Everything so right, so natural, so as it should be—until panic made a call on my mind and heart only days before the big event. There "he" was, and getting more intimidating with every thought, with every passing hour.

Soon, the cycle of fear kicked in; the episode became full-blown and here came the lie: *I can't do it.*

Everybody expected me to do it! I'd had over thirty years of pastoral experience and nearly as many years counseling. I'd taught counseling at the college level for eight years, addressing these issues in church, in class, in private session, on the radio, and in print. Somehow, I had gotten through the fray and the frazzle before—but not this time. This was my daughter's wedding. It was relationally "huge" and I hadn't come against these odds until then. I mean, the success of the whole memorable family testimonial fell basically on me to do my part. It would have been a disaster to choke, to melt down in embarrassment before an audience. Imagine the swirling thoughts, the cyclic thinking—moving faster and faster, while heightening the scare, the emotion, and the trauma I felt.

One thing became clear to me through the whole episode surrounding our family wedding: there was no out for me. God had put me in a strategic place of ministry and service. Avoidance, flight, or checking out were not options, which meant that if I continued with the same state of mind, well, I would bring the roof down on my head since the obstacle was just too daunting.

So I weighed the data and measured up all that was against me and who it was that was for me (Rom 8:31).[5] My flesh felt defeat, but my spirit cried, "Lord, I believe; help my unbelief!" (Mk 9:24).[6]

Off to the mountain I went and more than once, for I knew the one I would need to embrace in order to successfully confront the obstacle that lay before me. This was a faith issue. It was not an issue to avoid by taking a "happy" pill. The God that I served, the sovereign God in whom I had long declared and boasted, must come to my aid as He promised (Phlp 4:9).[7]

You see, my friend, the issue is never the real issue. The fear, the obstacle, the seemingly formidable odds is never the real problem. Problems and solutions are always about God. How sad it is that so many of us who profess to know the God of the Bible go through life without reckoning Jehovah as first cause. Life is intentional, and the event of this special occasion, among other things, was intended for prayer and for worship on my part (Eph 1:11).[8] The wedding was about Him, not about me. I became keenly aware of that with what was about to happen.

Few times has the Lord delivered me in the manner that He did. Usually, God has me work through an event. In the episode, I regularly apply the knowledge of God, utilizing those helps, methods, and weapons He has taught me. These subjects we will unpack later in our discussion. Specifically, on this occasion, complete victory over my fears met me in the prayer exercise itself. While I was seeking Jesus for help in the woods and on the hilltop alongside our home in the country, relief settled deep into my heart and nerves. When I rose to return to my duties, relief reigned and fear had flown from my mind. Soundness of mind set in with such strength that empathy for the other wedding participants ruled throughout the entire affair. There was not a rumble of confusion or even a quake of discomfort in my head.

There are those times when God simply flexes the muscle of His mercy and forgoes the rigor of battle needful to prove His own (2 Chron 20:17).[9] I see the value of the rigor, but if He chooses outright deliverance, well, that's cool. It makes me expect from Him, hope in Him, learn His ways, and welcome in faith how He shows Himself mighty before all odds. His name is El-Elyon, and He is the "Strongest Strong One." He alone is to be feared and believed (Ps 20:7).[10] By this knowledge, the fictitious myths of fear are exploited and the confidence that biblical faith augments is axiomatic or self-evident.

Chapter Two Endnotes

[1] Philippians 4:13. Learning contentedness amid upheavals and adverse situations is the preceding thought to the immediate verse. Paul muses, thus, upon the reality that Christ Himself strengthens the apostle in all that he does. Millions have rested upon this hope, just as the writer of this epistle.

² Romans 5:3, 4. "And not only that, but we also glory in tribulations. Knowing that tribulation produces perseverance, and perseverance, character, and character, hope." There is a certain glory in tribulations, troubles, and afflictions to produce by God's own Spirit definitive qualities of Christlikeness. Just as the wonder of Jesus' goodness is multidimensional and many-sided, so tribulations produce the "proven" grandeur of the divine nature by testing. The struggles come to all saints as they follow Christ and as they exude those many-tempered, communicable qualities owning to God Himself. Troubles are intended to translate into the "experience of hope" and in this respect the apostle Paul teaches that through affliction comes a real and genuine sense of rejoicing, boasting, or "glorying" in God.

³ First Samuel 17. This chapter of 1 Samuel essentially covers David's coming to fame before the eyes of all Israel and due, primarily, to his defeat of Goliath from Gath. The specific verse sightings are intended to document various aspects of the account throughout.

⁴ Hebrews 11:6. Verse 6 of Hebrews 11 is surely the key verse of all forty verses. The designation "Faith's Hall of Fame" is fitting to this disclosure of those who pleased God while in the flesh. Again, verse 6 reiterates the truth that diligent faith pleases the Almighty, so much so that God Himself is "the One who pays wages" (*misthapodotes*)—i.e., "rewarder," to those who seek Him out. Faith here and in the context should be seen as a verb to the reader, in a theological sense. In other words, the faith that pleases God is always active, earnest, and zealous for God, and it's consistent with the faith belonging to His elect. See Titus 1:1.

⁵ Romans 8:31. The preceding verses to this reference belong together as the great golden chain of redemption. They describe God's effectual working to bring about the salvation of His own. This work of God cannot be broken or undone. Spilling forth into verse 31, the apostle appears taken up with the experiential knowledge of divine purpose and thus challenges any and all doubt that might rival or rift the peace and security of those who belong to Christ.

⁶ Mark 9:24. The father of the child possessed by a demonic spirit voices his struggle to fully attend to the faith Jesus admonishes. "If you can believe, all things are possible to him who believes" (v. 23). Thank God that

ultimately healing is not dependent on the amount of faith, but upon the object of faith—even the Lord Himself. Faith struggles, but genuine faith perseveres despite all the smoke and warfare of the human heart and mind.

7 Philippians 4:9. Here lies a beautiful promise tucked among the joys of an inspiring epistle. The promise is God's own peace to those who act upon inspired doctrine.

8 Ephesians 1:11. The destiny of the elect is secured by divine purpose, thus "each and every"—i.e., *ta panta* (all) things that surround our lives are afforded only by God's volition/decreed action.

9 2 Chronicles 20:17. The scene is warfare and the hostile invasion of the peoples of Moab and Ammon, together with the Ammonites, against King Jehoshaphat (v.1). The Bible speaks of a great multitude "which had advanced near En Gedi." Jeshoshaphat feared, but "set himself to seek the Lord, and proclaimed a fast" (v.3). The response of Jehovah to the cry of His people was outright deliverance. . . "You will not need to fight in this battle. Position yourselves, stand still and see the salvation of the Lord" (v. 17). Though not generally the case, God may in some situations demonstrate His power and presence by simply exempting His children from the normal escape route, which is the fire walk of affliction.

10 Psalm 20:7. Obviously, Israel used chariots and horses in defense of her homeland. The use of means like that of a stave or sling is not sinful in and of itself, but trusting in them or putting one's confidence in them more than strong reliance upon the Lord is simply misplaced hope. The "Name of the Lord our God," upon which God's people rely, is not to be understood as a chant or some magical litany. The phrase is to be construed as the divine personage, meriting one's absolute dependence.

CHAPTER 3

Contacts, Connections, and Counsel

So what goes on with a fear episode, a fear event? The one who experiences the problem knows the fear as all too real. Any attempts by counselors, whether Christian or secular, to minimize what is actual, only serve to hinder the helping process. Counseling experience demonstrates that to be true.

Basic Mechanics

Earlier, we said that the phobic episode may have a diversity of links, or stimuli, but, at its core, the symptoms are similar and calculated. The stages of fear are:

First: the Sensory Fix—The Intake

In this first stage of phobia, certain stimuli trigger distraction in the normal flow of thinking so that a "fix" or focus occurs. It may be a visible fix, such as an animal, a bridge, a crowd, darkness, elevators, fire, etc., or a combination of these that incites diversionary attention in our mind.

It might be a smell, an aroma, or a scent that grabs the attention of a person, drawing his or her thoughts to some associational connect; it is usually linked with some fearful situation out of the past.

Possibly, it's auditory. Once we come in contact again with "that sound," a link to a "bad experience" occurs, stimulating an undue or overdone fixation with the sudden noise or other auditory intake.

It may be taste that aggravates the cycle of fear, drawing out of our memory a situation from the past. Although the history may be hardly clear, lucid, or evident in our thoughts—the panic, the discomfort we felt somewhere in the past is vividly etched into our minds. What we taste is the link to fear.

Finally, there is the touch factor. This sense picks up the stimulus and follows along the groove of association until fear surfaces, like the man who, feeling the texture of a sock left in his bed while sleeping, awakened to a full-blown episode with a "cottonmouth snake." Until help came and the lights went on, the snake was very real as the desperate soul, in great earnest, held the "snake" at bay for what seemed like an eternity. The feel of an object can result in a trigger, whereby fear shows up in startling fashion.

Second: Adrenal Hype—The Alarm

The next stage of the fear encounter is the issue of an adrenal response accentuated by the sensory stimuli. Sometimes it appears that the jolt, start, or alarm that we feel comes so automatically that clients have suggested they had no cognitive interaction with the stimuli (i.e., there was certainly no "reason" for it); the impulse simply "caught me by surprise." If an individual becomes convinced that fear events "just happen," the healing/helping process may be complicated by self-fulfilling prophecy, namely, "It simply happens; it's out of my control, and I'm victimized by the disease or disorder." It is so easy for the sufferer to pick up secular labels in this regard and, sadly, wear them. "Alas, our frailty is the cause, not we!"[1] Reason may not be involved since the reflex is habituated. In practical terms, our brains have flagged or bookmarked a former bad experience; so, together with the sensory link, we are conditioned for the hype, for the exaggerated element of fear. The truth is, we have thought about the link before, and it troubles us. We are very good about remembering our "traumas"—so good, in fact, that they are all filed among our staple reactions. There was just no plan in place to do anything else with the data but panic. As long as that precedent and pattern exists in our heads, we will become good at doing the wrong thing every time. Adrenal hype is what we might expect in the fear experience. The immensity of the problem is always dependent upon to what extent a person has left the hype unchallenged, cognitively. Adrenaline/epinephrine serves us well to stimulate our heart, promote muscle strength, and prepare us for a heightened performance. God intended such hormones to assist us, and yet, if we draw upon their supply without sound reason, behavioral controls are thrown to the wind and the exhibition may be unwanted. There's always a lot of "hype" along the pathway to fear, and adrenaline is ready to give a boost to either the rational or the irrational signal. The habituated signal of a sound mind is intended of God to prevail upon behavior (2 Tim 1:7;[2] Rom 6:14).[3]

It has been my practice as a pastor to ask those who are fearful to pray publicly (those who seek to avoid small group meetings out of psychological discomfort or opt out of a whole spectrum of service opportunities because of the emotional hype they hear "inside") how they intend to move through all the flak. Life is simply all over the place. The fire of antiaircraft guns is clamorous, strong, and opposing. The question is, "How?" "What?" is the strategy we will employ to maximize our lives as overcomers. Adrenal hype is there; it comes from all over—wherever, whenever. A "no plan" is conditioned defeat and a pattern for spiritual delinquency.

Third: Cognitive Chaos—The Eclipse

Thoughts are everywhere: exaggerated thoughts, thoughts that eclipse sound reason. In every observable case, the sort of thinking that appears to be gaining momentum in the fear event is the worst scenario stuff: the extreme, the Murphy's Law syndrome.

Here, where the thought process becomes so congested and so overwhelmed, is where we feel hemmed in with no escape route save the irrational exit. The following are some illustrations of exit thinking—bizarre ways from real-life accounts, in which some folks have succumbed to fear:

- "I thought about jumping from the Ferris wheel."
- "I contemplated jumping overboard and swimming to shore."
- "I wash all my money to avoid the contamination of germs."

Then, there was a court advocate who panicked when he, ironically, was summoned to a court appearance. He resolved to flee the state as his only possible solution. Even the mere discussion of his court appearance brought nervous and unusual contortions to the man's face.

Finally, there was an episode when this author heard his name announced over the public address system as "on deck" for the next wrestling match in the gymnasium. In that moment of time, fear showed up at mat side. I hadn't seen him for nearly twenty-five years, but at forty-four years of age, in a seniors' tournament, there was some sensory fix, some psyche-physic alarm, and some mental confusion that prompted me to peruse the exit doors for an escape—to make a mad dash to the car, with or without my manager (who happened to be my then-sixteen-year-old son)! Well, thankfully, through the sufficient Spirit and practical insight into the ways and means of grace, the challenge was met. The opponent was defeated and victory was whole and complete. In reflection, the entire event is a good memory for both my soul and my son, whose pastoral work lends much counseling.

Fourth and Final: Cyclic Fright—The Spiral

The best description I can give for this phase is that of a cyclone. The spinning motion of the storm picks up debris as its circular movement intensifies. The devastating effects of the cyclone are graduated by the tossing forth of its twisted and turning collections.

Diagram 3
The Fright Cycle: The Downward Trend

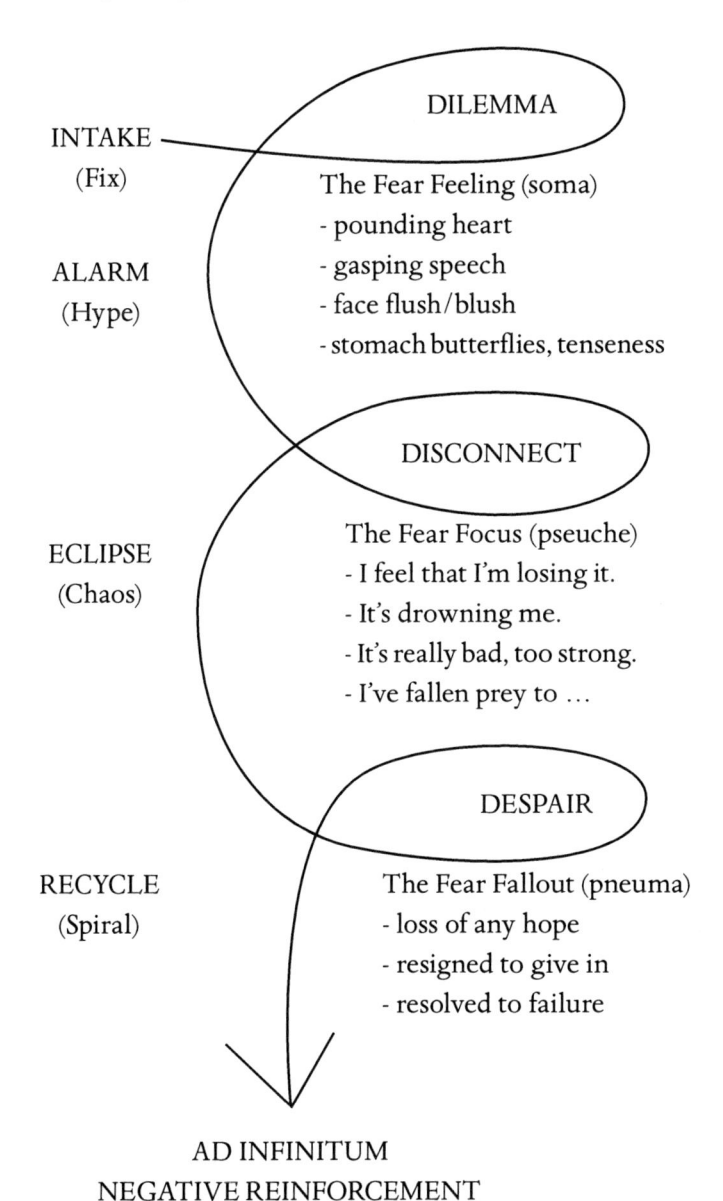

INTAKE
(Fix)

DILEMMA

The Fear Feeling (soma)
- pounding heart
- gasping speech
- face flush/blush
- stomach butterflies, tenseness

ALARM
(Hype)

DISCONNECT

The Fear Focus (pseuche)
- I feel that I'm losing it.
- It's drowning me.
- It's really bad, too strong.
- I've fallen prey to …

ECLIPSE
(Chaos)

DESPAIR

The Fear Fallout (pneuma)
- loss of any hope
- resigned to give in
- resolved to failure

RECYCLE
(Spiral)

AD INFINITUM
NEGATIVE REINFORCEMENT

Thoughts, spiraling out of control, gain strength as the fearful one focuses on the cycle itself. Once the panic is full-blown, all "eyes" are on the details of the storm, the feelings of the fear, and all the hype of the episode. What is happening is cyclic fright, and round and round we go—fearing the fear, frightful of the feeling, and enabling a debilitating pattern of existence—like the little merry-go-rounds at the park that we spin with our children hanging on, reinforcing their excitement (or scare) by the rapidity of the spinning motion.

At this stage, any or all of the following can become very pronounced: perspiration, dryness of mouth, difficulty breathing and swallowing, muscle tension, irritability, anger, a queasy stomach, a pounding heart, mental lapses, etc. The heightened awareness of what is going on in our mind and body only serves to feed the storm and lengthen the event. There is simply far too much focus on "what is happening," rather than rational assessment and solutions, reasonable probes and plotting. The direction of this cycle of fright always trends downward.

Sophists and Circuitry

Only recently, I tuned in to a series of late-night discussions on the subject of the brain, hosted by noted journalist and largely political commentator, Charlie Rose. The guests for this PBS broadcast were world-renowned professors, neurologists, psychiatrists, scientists, and other brilliant minds, who labored, no doubt, to articulate their finds to the common viewer.[4]

The information gathered from medical science and the decades of research was fascinating and, in many cases, insightful and helpful. Besides provoking my worship of such an amazing God, I left the program quite humbled at my impoverished knowledge of such a spectacular piece of genius—the human brain!

It did not take very long, however, to catch the bias of the natural man, of the natural mind. There has been a growing air of omniscience in medical science that denies any idea that the immaterial part of man affects or impacts upon human behavior. Although I do not pretend to be credentialed as our PBS panelists, it did not take a rocket scientist to gather the clear and present lesson of this broadcast. Let me summarize the dominant lyric and obvious lesson:

> Once we thought that human beings had a soul which performed functions we could not explain, but now we know that all of these functions are simply the activity of the brain.

Sound familiar? It is but the resonate theme of today's medical opinion. An opinion which attempts to explain the link between the human species and their behavior.

In short, medical science concludes that there is no soul, no immaterial part of humans that affects behavior. Physical matter—this is what we are and all we are—is the final analysis. Suggestions that we are something else are unacceptable, paranormal, and even "wrong" by the standards of the contemporary medical model. We might call this approach reductionism, practical atheism, or an idea that "behind every crooked thought there is a crooked molecule" (Welch, p. 15).[5]

Now, how do you treat a crooked molecule? With a pill, of course, or, possibly, some Pavlovian technique that might condition neurotransmitters to reroute, alleviating the unpleasantries of, let's say, a frightful episode. Observation tells us, pragmatically speaking, that it works. Symptoms can usually be suppressed. After all, life can go on. Band-Aids are useful when "you haven't got time for the pain," when life is all "sound and fury, signifying nothing" (Shakespeare)[6]. The evidence should not be surprising, but when discussing the pervasive use of mood-altering drugs, my doctor recently commented that I would be shocked to see how many in our small community reported regular use of psychotropics on their PDI (personal data information) records.

When visiting another physician with whom I have been a long standing patient, this doctor concurred that psychotropic medication for anxiety, panic, or bottom-line fear episodes (DSM—"disorders") is monumental, widespread, and extensive. "We've got to do something else," said my physician. Frankly, I have long been an advocate for a viable cure! No, not a pain free existence, but help beyond those symptom patch jobs and mindless fixes that have no connection to wholeness, to purpose, to growth, or to godliness.

> Come to Me, all you that labor and are heavy laden, and I will give you rest. Take My yoke upon you and learn from Me, for I am gentle and lowly in heart, and you will find rest for your souls. (Mt 11:28, 29)[7]

While studying the text of First Corinthians 15 for a Sunday exposition that I was sharing with believers, I ran across an interesting find by Dr. Gordon H. Clark. Theologian, linguist, and scholar, Dr. Clark distinguishes the contrast of the natural body versus the spiritual body as delineated by the apostle Paul in this great resurrection chapter, "If 'natural' denoted the faculty of sensation, 'spiritual' would have to mean, rational."

Clark goes on to say, "Taken at face value, this means that in our present life, we have sensations, but no reason. This means that the image of God, if man was, indeed, created in God's image, was not merely depraved or defaced, but annihilated by the fall ..."[8] Perhaps, this was the revelation Jesus was giving to His disciples when He used *anoetoc* (mindless) in reference to their thinking (Lk 24:25).[9]

Human beings do not reason well. Despite the innovative gains in modern technology, mankind does not reason well in his moral judgments. Characterizing the latter days of human history just prior to the Second Advent of Jesus Christ, prophetic words underscore the predominate state of mind in society at large: "Always learning and never able to come to the knowledge of the truth" (2 Tim 3:7).[10] Apparently, and as Jesus demonstrates with His disciples, even the followers of Christ can fall into patterns of the natural man and fail to image God in their minds.

Irrational fear needs to be challenged at its core. Irrational fear needs to be addressed in the "being" aspect of living souls. Fear is a faith issue, for "whatever is not from faith, is sin" (Rom 14:23).[11] Life is intended to force the issue upon us. Life has purpose, and God has decreed the experience of our existence as the proving ground of our trust and confidence (Ps 11:4, 5;[12] Jer 17:10).[13] The shepherd boy's success in battle grew out of his private reliance upon the God who is there; the confrontation only confirmed this reality. David reasoned morally and fought well. In practice, David was no atheist. He was spiritually adept (Rev 1:17b).[14]

Chapter Three Endnotes

[1] Edward T. Welch, Counselors Guide to the Brain and Its Disorders (Zondervon Publishing House: Grand Rapids, 1991), 15.

[2] Second Timothy 1:7. Although the Greek term for fear is not *phobos*, but *deilia* in the immediate verse, general "fright" is implied—whether timidity, cowardice, or simply choosing to be afraid. Paul would dissuade Timothy from fear in the ministry, a fear that would be aggravated by hostile hearers, censure of the state, or clamor from the crowds. W. E. Vine rightly said, "That spirit [fearfulness] is not given us of God." (*Vine's Expository Dictionary of New Testament Words*, Vol. 2, p. 84.)

[3] Romans 6:14. This verse is used to demonstrate that there is enablement through God's grace to choose the good over the bad, the righteous habit over the unrighteous, faith over fear. Plainly, sinning is a choice of the will. Where God's grace resides, believers are freed to exercise mastery over the flesh by the action of the will.

[4] *The Brain.* Interview by Charlie Rose (PBS network with leading panelist, Eric Kendel, Tuesday, May 29, 2012), internet accessed June 23, 2013.

5 Edward T. Welch, *Counselors Guide to the Brain and Its Disorders* (Zondervon Publishing House, Grand Rapids, 1991), 15.

6 William Shakespeare, *Macbeth*. Editors Barbara Mowat, Paul Werstine (Washington Press: NY, 1992).

7 Matthew 11:28–30. Upon reproving the unbelief of several cities where Jesus had wrought mighty works and after passing judgment on them, our Lord extends an invitation to the weary, to those burdened down with care. He teaches clearly that relief for afflicted souls can be found in the person of the Master, even Jesus Christ Himself. Here, He cites the cure for all human care and distress. It is evident, however, by the preceding verse that the reality of this blessed boon is known only to those whom the Father has *"apo* [from] *kalupto* [cover]," or to those minds that the Father has "uncovered" Him [Christ]. In short, if you've beheld Jesus in a salvific way, you have beheld the absolute and objective solution to all perplexity of heart and mind. Not that the believing soul is freed from struggle or from the smoke and warfare of the practical human dilemma, but freed from the control of those oppressive elements of human despair and hopelessness.

8 Gordon Clark, *1 Corinthians* (Jefferson, Maryland: The Trinity Foundation, 1975), 299, 300.

9 Luke 24:25. "O, mindless ones," declares Jesus to the perplexed disciples traveling the Emmaus Road. Despite all the lessons of life and lips from the greatest of all teachers, His followers just didn't get it. They could not reason well due to their innate depravity; this truth underscores man's desperate need for God's own Spirit (1 John 3).

10 Second Timothy 3:7. The truth that is in Jesus contrasts the mere educational and technological advancements of mankind. The observations of the experts may indeed be helpful, but somewhere in their conclusions they will be amiss, for there is, without Christ, a dimension to life they will never see, thus their finds will always be incongruous and incoherent. You simply cannot know osmosis without moral reason. Here is the substance of human blindness and depravity so often at the heart of Christ's teaching.

11 Romans 14:23. Irrational fears do not flow from the perspective of a heart stayed on Jehovah. The jolt or start from stimuli is the knee-jerk reaction to life coming at us, but, like any other temptation, what becomes of it? In other words, how do we choose to deal with it—in faith, or in fright? Choices become habituated routines and they are telling on us, for, as someone has so aptly said, "It is not what we think we are, but it is what we think, we are!"

12 Psalm 11:4, 5. "His eyes behold, His eyelids test the sons of men," and the text goes on to say that even the righteous—but especially the righteous—are tested of the Lord. In fact, God's testing is certain testament to His dominion from the heavens.

13 Jeremiah 17:10. This is one of the clearest teachings, in first person, where God discloses His relentless pursuit of man to prove the motivations of the soul through providential pressure. Essential holiness compels the Almighty to a ruthless pursuit of all idolatry. Essential love compels the Almighty to the remedy of a cross for all idol worshippers (Rom 6:23).

14 Revelation 1:17b. "[D]o not afraid: I am the First and the Last …" The experiential knowledge of the only true and living God gave speed to David's aggression on the battleground. Truly, "hoofing it" was a statement of David's faith in Jehovah.

CHAPTER 4

Matters of Management and Mastery

There is the sort of theological misconception today that suggests that divine promise ensures the removal of affliction. Indomitable faith is seen as the answer of ultimate peace and riddance from the smoke and warfare Satan precipitates in the human heart. In this vein of reason, the friction, frazzle, and fray of fear have been annihilated by the cross of Christ and can be banished on command by the stalwart, the strong, and the Spirit-filled. Now, frankly, I do not believe this tenant to be true or sound, either by Scripture or by experience.

In teaching God's Word in an expository format, I have a rich appreciation for the language of the Bible and the contextual sense of things. There is so very much that can go adrift in biblical hermeneutics when careful, contextual study is not the staple of our search for the true sense of any given passage. In all my finds, however, I have never known any biblical promise to give even the notion that a believer may, in this life, reach a plateau of spiritual maturity where he or she can become exempt from the fear struggle, or better said, the faith struggle. In fact, this is how growth comes to us; it is largely born out of struggle.

Everywhere we look in God's creation, there is testament to the principle of effort, strain, stretching, and pulling until the destination or divine intention is complete. In the redemptive purpose of God, struggle has always been part of the plan. Affliction, combat, and even ongoing warfare is a matter of decree (and degree).

The good and the bad elements of life act as planing tools to perfect in us certain qualities of wisdom that are intended to equip us more sensibly, relationally, spiritually, and effectually as human beings. This revelation should be especially known to those who have been awakened to God by the regenerating effect of the Holy Spirit (Eph 2:1–10;[1] Jn 3:1–21).[2] The benefits of the struggling and the wrestling are many, but they come to us by the process of exertion, just as creation illustrates in the transformation of the caterpillar to a butterfly.

May I suggest the struggle itself as a gift from God? So why are we bent upon eliminating the process with dependencies such as a chemical fix, a mood-altering drug (prescription or not), a caffeine high or proof spirit? (Just a question, not a condemnation—only a logical, reflective question, if our premise is accurate.)

God's intention is that we master our fears by smart wrestling, by lucid aggression at every turn, time and time again. Experience tells us there will be defeats and mishaps, but there is enablement and there will be management. About the dividends, the benefits—they will be maximized because you have suffered, you have been stretched. You, by God's enabling grace, have gained a dimension of faith that you could not have learned any other way. Herein is the design of the assay.

Insights from 1 Corinthians 10:1

The Scripture surrounding our immediate text has to do with the wilderness people, the children of Israel. It is a picture of the nation's struggle with trials and temptations. From this illustration, we receive both example and admonition: example of what not to do and admonition as to what God would have us do.

Again, it is all in the context of testing. Smack dab in the middle of the admonition to deny sin and honor the Savior, we have a wonderful promise of comfort and hope. There is no question that God has high expectations for obedience in the lives of His people, but, praise His name, the Lord always supplies enablement with His commands. Consider for a moment:

The Nature of the Temptation

So what kind of temptation are we talking about? Is the temptation spoken of here relative to our discussion of fear? This word *temptation* is used twice in our verse and is the common language term *peirasmos*. This same word, also translated "to test" or "trial," is used elsewhere in the New Testament. See Matthew 22:18 (test);[3] James 1:2 (trials), v. 13 (tempt) NKJV.[4]

W. E. Vine does a very good job delineating the term and its use in any given text, but I found Richard's and MacArthur's insight most helpful to our subject:

> A temptation is a difficult situation, a pressure that brings a reaction through which the character or commitment of the believer is demonstrated.[5]

> [E]very difficult circumstance that enters a believer's life can either strengthen him if he obeys God and remains confident in His care, or become a solicitation to evil if the believer chooses, instead, to doubt God and disobey His Word.[6]

The Scripture before us is certainly applicable to our discussion of fear as a temptation, a test-tempt. The faceoff with any situation that would draw away our peace and reliance upon Jesus Christ is exactly what 1 Corinthians 10:13 drives home.

Furthermore, the nature of the temptation is said to be "overtaking." The original sense of this Greek word implies to capture or arrest, to lay hold of, and suggests power or force.

Obviously, the entrapment of irrational fear is not of God, for

"[W]hatsoever is not of faith, is sin" (Rom. 14:23).[7] Neither does God entice human beings to sin, "for God cannot be tempted by evil, nor does He Himself tempt anyone [to evil]" (James 1:13).[8]

Clearly, ownership for irrational fear rests squarely upon human beings, while the force to be reckoned with—the source of intrusion that compels us to surrender or collapse spiritually—is ultimately inner depravity. Inner depravity, or the Adamic nature, which the Bible refers to as the "old man," "futile mind," etc., is the latch-string of all devilish intervention.

James declared that one is "drawn away by his own desires" (James 1:14),[9] while Jesus taught that Satan was actively seeking to sift or winnow Peter's heart and character (Luke 22:31).[10] Truly, mastery over debilitating phobias involves habituating sound, biblical thinking, and latching the door of our minds from the inside. In this way, we can curtail the inroads of outside influences (2 Cor 10:3–6;[11] James 4:7).[12]

The nature of temptation, then, speaks both of victim and victimizing. A frightful situation may arise from anywhere, anyplace, and at any time. We are not always in control of life events. The solicitation to evil, however, will come against us from within and without, targeting the very areas of our vulnerability. Evil's march into our minds calls for management and mastery, since the power of choice is always resident in the sound mind (Rom 6:14).[13]

A Case and a Point

In but a few verses from the Gospel of Mark, we again find so much help relative to the fear/faith struggle! Beginning at verse 37 of Mark, chapter 4, we find a windstorm on the Sea of Galilee and a frightened bunch of disciples feverishly trying to keep their wits about them amid a listing fishing vessel. The Sea of Galilee is known for its hostile tempests (due primarily to its shallow depth and geography that produces a wind tunnel effect upon the water). Storms get violent—fast!

The original language here is quite descriptive. It was a "storm of wind." The wind is described as "great" from the Greek word, *megas*, sometimes translated "violent." So a violent storm of wind was descending upon this low-lying *thalassa* (a great expanse of water).

Certainly, the stimuli for fear are all there in full force. There's the howling wind, the boisterous waves hurling their weight against fragile resistance, blinding mist, and the turbulent sensation of a small, listing, heaving *ploion* (ship with a sail). In this classical usage, this term might apply to any sized sailing vessel. So here, in its common occurrence, the term "ship" is accurately rendered (although, boat is more appropriate to the modern reader).

But where is the Master in this oppressive gale? Why, He's asleep (verse 38)! Jesus is in a deep sleep, worn out from His vigorous ministry routine, no doubt.

Truly, it is a fright-filled situation for the disciples—the storm catching them by surprise, else they would not have ventured out into the deep.

We know from the story line that the followers of Jesus are being tempted toward irrational fear. We know this because of their frantic waking of the Master with the words, "Teacher, do You not care that we are perishing?" This is a prime example of frenzied reproof, or a judgmental inquiry—a question where fear seems to override the reasonable, rational and truthful.

The question is, in reality, a statement of unbelief. That is exactly why the sovereign God, who is obviously watching over His Son, brought the disciples into the tempest. The episode at Galilee is a test-tempt—a solicitation to evil from the Adversary, but the proving ground of faith for the followers of Jesus.

The natural mind of the disciples was vulnerable to the inroads of evil enticement. Instead of confronting their fears with the truth, these ordinary regulars yielded to the winnowing of the wild and untenable. Although they did not fully understand exactly just who it was that slept so peacefully in the stern, nevertheless, they had walked with the Master and they were well acquainted with

His ways. Yet, when the lion roared, they flinched and aroused the Lord with the words (literal translation), "Teacher, is it no concern to You that we perish?"

Unreasonable, irrational, defamatory! The latch-string of inward depravity exhaled, inhaling a foul spirit that flew directly into the face of God. Faith was the issue. Faith was the only way to manage the moment.

How interesting to meditate upon the lesson of our text. As Jesus adjudged the wind (a term I prefer to best express the Creator's command of calm), peace ensued immediately!

The awe-stricken subjects of the King come to terms with the wonder that God was in the boat. Gripping fear, fear that erased all hope and loosed all the moorings of a sound mind, was replaced with a holy, righteous, and healthy fear of the sovereign God.

In both cases—in the matter (natural elements) and in the mind—peace and solace returned. What a find! What a lesson! The fear of Jehovah was great, exceedingly great, so much so that it overruled the seemingly overpowering onslaught.

Don't miss it! The point of our text is a gem. The fear of God overcomes, yea, overwhelms the fear(s) of man! Once faith lays hold of the wonder and knowledge of God, the storm is embraced with calm resolve and solid assurance.

Indeed, these soldiers of Jesus have many more battles ahead of them. God would pursue them faithfully to their appointed struggles. There were more temptations, more testing and trials from everyplace, anywhere, and at any time.

Our Lord's words would fall upon their hearts again and again: "Why are you fearful, O you of little faith?" (Matt 8:26).[14] Observers at the scene of the cross, witnessing the tragic event and the cowering of the frightened band of dispersed followers, could have concluded Jesus' lessons all failures. Repetition does breed retention, but even this academic maxim seemed beyond the ability of our Lord's sluggish students.

The event of Calvary was not the end of it all, as we well know.

Divine motivation, "not many days hence (Acts 2),"[15] would thrust God's regulars into a renewed passion for the friction, fray, and frazzle of the "good fight." The fight, though, is relentless. It is the fight to pursue God's glory by the tenacious exercise of conformity to the very image and likeness of faith's victor, even Jesus Christ (Rom 8:29).[16]

In the journey before them, men of God would emerge: no, not perfect men, but men who were prepared and well exercised in the management of their baser fears, men who were becoming more skillful in the battle for a whole, healthy, sound mind.

A Pertinent Illustration

It was my senior year of college. I was finishing up my wrestling career with one loss on the season and poised to win Nationals. My only loss came against an All-American, who would later place fourth in the Division II tournament. Honestly, I was flying high, feeling good, ready to rumble—until I got my wings clipped in a match only a week before tournament time.

Since that day, I've shared with only a few the real story behind the loss. You certainly wouldn't want to tell your opponent what happened. And your teammates, well, it might appear to them as an excuse, so—drop it; stuff it. And I did, for years.

The truth is, I choked that night. I stumbled, panicked. The stimulus was Popeye arms. That's right. I noticed my opponent's arms and started thinking irrationally: *Suppose he holds me down, gives me a tight waist so that I can't breathe? What if I panic? Will I scream for the referee to stop the match? Will I go insane and kick, bite ...?*

The more I listened to myself, the more my opponent gained advantage until I pinned myself. I actually telegraphed the move I was going to use so my competitor could plan on seizing a quick pin and end the match. It worked. It worked so effectively that I lost my next match in this triangular meet for lack of concentration; two losses, same day—out of fear.

So what do you do? Is there a choice? Was I going to honor God, fulfill my commitment to the team, to the school, and to mastery over my fears? Personally, could I continue to enable the cycle of fear? Whatever the outcome, I chose to lace up my sneakers and battle temptation. If not here, the line would be drawn somewhere, someplace, some other time.

On to our tourney I went, humbly entreating God and challenging every thought that threatened my gravity of mind. Interestingly, my rival for the championship was very upper body, but this time I did not hesitate. I fully committed myself to the business at hand. Sheer grit, right? No. Resolve? Yes, but reliance—reliance upon the God who brought me back to the circle and enabled me to exercise my faith in Him alone.

Now, just in case you wonder about God's attention to detail in the growth process, listen to this one. Years later, I told my wife that this particular loss still plagued me; I had never forgotten my competitor's name. So my wife suggested that I google him and find out for myself who he is, where he is—(you gotta understand, this quest was a wrestler thing, i.e., vain rudiments). I googled him and, sure enough, there he was, an artist. Among his accomplishments read this accolade, "Hall of Fame Wrestler." Oh, yes, that explains my loss. There must have been more to the story—please tell me there was some justification to my fear!

The next thing I did was to send off an e-mail, and the response came as a rebuke to my nominal way of thinking. "Mark Graham," he said. "I remember you; you were the winner, I was the loser," he replied. "You see, I had no time for God in my life while a student at the university, and you trained as a pastor and have been serving all these years."

I think that was pretty much his text, but it spoke volumes to my heart. What is most important in life? What was I thinking, again? Surely, God reminded me once more, the fray was about Him. It always is! What He was doing in those nine minutes (or in that case, eight minutes) was intended for His glory in the lives of both contestants.

Guess I need to communicate with my friend once more on a higher plane. I had no idea that the frazzle would incite an open door forty years later. Amazing detail. Amazing God. He even uses failures to His glorious end. Up to the fray! Don't miss God's game plan.

But back to our Corinthian text—there's another find worth rediscovering! The nature of our temptation is said to have a reputation of commonality. In general, the obstacles that human beings face in life are ordinary, or such as "belong to man," as the language implies.

In other words, there is no such thing as a purely unique temptation. Our reaction to given stimuli may spin a tale in our minds that what we are facing, what we are battling, cannot be understood by anyone else, since it is outside the realm of the ordinary. It is simply unusual, queer, and strange, out of the way of anything others could lucidly grasp. Remember again, the stimuli are diverse, and their types, combinations, and arrays may appear somewhat unique to each combatant; but the feel of the fear episode, with its flurry, its flush, and its fury, is ordinary. It has all the components of what we know come against other human beings!

Take heart—common temptations befall us all. Everyone feels the jolt with something, somewhere, sometime. So don't get hung up with psychological labels, for they just might become a self-fulfilling prophecy. Sincere Christians need encouragement to do battle with this understanding:

> Casting all your care upon Him, for He cares for you. Be sober, be vigilant; because your adversary the devil walks about like a roaring lion, seeking whom he may devour. Resist him, steadfast in the

> faith, knowing that the *same sufferings* [author's emphasis]are experienced by your brotherhood in the world. (II Pe 5:7-9)[17]

There is nothing suggested from the context that "sufferings" here, is to be relegated to the persecuted saint only. Sometimes rendered "afflictions" elsewhere, they encompass the whole lot of what flies against our faith and our reliance upon God. All humanity suffers, and believers find no exemption to what befalls the cosmos of worldlings. Yet we are admonished by Peter to glorify God in our sufferings as Christians (1 Pe 4:16).[18] The logic of good hermeneutics finds application for the suffering we experience from the world, from the flesh, or from the Devil. Each category is a battleground of suffering and affliction, and each calls for the same readiness that has characterized other victorious brethren in the fray.

Finally, and most notably, our verse teaches us that God is faithful to provide a way out of every temptation without us collapsing! Inferred in our text is the thought that the escape comes amid, or better, *through* the conflict—not apart from it. God can be counted on to bear us up under the temptation. Herein is the escape! This insight is consistent with the most literal rendering of the Greek word, *hupophero,* (to bear up under). Endurance is the quality of abiding under suffering, difficulty, or hardship. This is exactly the escape hatch the apostle has in mind in 1 Corinthians 10:13. Dominance over fear comes by learning to endure it, not by running from it, and never by seeking to avoid it!

Savor this gem from Philippians 4:9,[19] where Paul admonishes his audience to apply the lessons from the life and lips of the apostle as the means to ensure peace of mind.

This is not intended to suggest some mindless, transcendent exercise for inner conscious tranquility. It is a call, rather, to obedience, to biblical teaching and doctrine resulting in godly behavior. Paul beckons us to do what we have learned, received, heard, and seen in his own life. In the actual activity of faith, "the God of peace will be with you."

Practically speaking, we must fight to keep the peace! There's no mastery without maneuvering, no proficiency without practice, no endurance without effort, and no deliverance without doing. "[T]hese *do* and the God of peace will be with you" (Phil. 4:9).

Faltering under the burden of trials is always self-inflicted, for the promise of 1 Corinthians 10:13 hones in on God's own faithfulness as the modus operandi of all endurance (cp. Phlp 2:12, 13).[20] The activity of faith brings the most pleasure to God. We could have no clearer applause of this truth than Hebrews, chapter 11. God not only delights in the good fight, but incites it, upholds us in it, and rewards us for enjoining it (Phlp 3:12–15;[21] 2 Tim 4:4–8!)[22]

The last few years, I have begun to develop an aversion for larger boats or smaller dinner cruise type ships. A couple of times on vacation, the discussion has come up between my wife, Diane, and me about a dinner cruise or sight-seeing excursion. I'm skilled, of course, at changing the subject when I'm trying to avoid something. My lovely wife is skilled, as well, in bringing me back into the circle.

Now, the stimulus can be so unpredictable. After all, I have my little fishing boat and often traverse the lakes of central New York to "catch a yarn or two" for my grandchildren. But ask me to go for a St. Lawrence Seaway excursion and I'll have to opt out.

I've thought about the aversion more carefully of late and, yes, there is an associational link. Years ago, I had gone on a dinner cruise with my wife and I had been jarred once or twice with the thought of just how quickly, or not, I'd be able to get to shore if I felt the jolt of a fear episode.

These were but passing thoughts, way back when, but they had brought me some discomfort, some annoyance, and a light harassment that I have never forgotten. So, avoidance. My wife knew it and she never pressed it; besides, there were alternatives to a date-night anniversary cruise. Not a big deal, until some dear friends made a visit to our home and wanted to take us out for a cruise on the St. Lawrence. You know, Bolt Castle, Singer Castle—the whole seven hour thing by boat.

We enjoy wonderful Christian fellowship with this family, and I knew that mutual edification would characterize our time together. Since the family was now living in Florida and only in our area for a brief time before dropping off their college-bound daughter, obviously, I could not allow fear to rule the day. The real clincher to the scenario lay in the fact that I was on the downhill stretch in writing the book you are now reading!

Once I conceded to what God had put on the table, I was resolved to rejoice in the greater opportunity of love and engage the challenge. In short, it was a most wonderful event. After committing the whole affair to God, fleshing out my plan for combat, and enlisting the support and accountability of my wife and guests, we sailed smoothly upon the peaceful seas of God's grace. There was no incident, only an occasional, fleeting dart that never lodged in my head.

And you know what? You guessed it—how soon can we go again? A good memory, a faithful God, endurance, and once again a life not deprived of golden opportunities.

Listening to a radio discussion on the use of psychotropic drugs a few years ago, I was, again, disappointed with the advice of a well-known Christian psychologist. In response to the question whether or not it was sinful for Christians to use meds for the treatment of conditions such as fear and panic, the counselor immediately retorted that "it might be sinful not to take them."

Because I understood this counselor's background and training, I anticipated his answer, but such a response needed to be couched in a biblical context. The wisdom of God's Word should have taught him to give clarity to the question. There's just too much to be gained from the challenge of a fear encounter. There are simply too many lessons that are tossed to the wind by an easy forfeit.

Personal, clear-eyed involvement with our struggles is the best way to achieve the dividends of wisdom and increasing faith.

Besides, I would have never known the raw import of Psalm 46:1[23] without the prostrate heart and mind: "God is our refuge and strength, a very present help in trouble." The sweetness of that intimate knowledge is reflected in Job's declaration: "For I know that my Redeemer lives" (Job 19:25).[24]

There's something synthetic about lifting up a prayer to God for our monetary needs while intending to call our rich aunt and share the prayer request. This sort of high level begging takes the expectation out of faith in God alone! Learning to manage our daily cares with the converting power of God's law (Ps 19:7)[25] brings mastery to life itself, building a quality of faith reflective of Christ's very mind.

> Therefore, preparing your minds for action, and being sober minded, set your hope fully on the grace that will be brought to you at the revelation of Jesus Christ. (1 Pe 1:13 ESV)[26]

Chapter Four Endnotes

[1] Ephesians 2:1–10. The passage is descriptive of God's work in the transformation of the sinner's life. It also demonstrates the modus of the unregenerate life, which is essentially self-serving. In specific, this portion of the epistle illustrates the change in one who is made alive by God to realities of His Spirit. The text pictures a "grace event," which brings about the radical spiritual change in the life of the believing soul. The change becomes evident by good works, in contrast to the disobedient desires of the past life (while discounting any good work as meritorious). The transformation is seen to be by grace alone through faith, resulting in a life change that is credited to God's workmanship.

[2] John 3:1–21. The well-known teaching of Jesus contained here uncovers the movement of the Holy Spirit in giving spiritual life to the natural heart. The life of God's Spirit is afforded through the message of Christ's atoning passion and by the appropriation of that message to one's own life by faith

alone (v. 16). Jesus Christ credits the whole matter of one's spiritual birth to the Holy Spirit and describes the soul's renewal as being "born from above" (from "ano"—i.e., a higher place). Spirit birth enables the recipient to embrace unseen realities, divine purpose, and redemptive meaning behind the seemingly casual accident of life.

[3] Matthew 22:18. *Peirasmos* is here rendered "test," and it is used in reproof by Jesus toward those Pharisees who "plotted how they might entangle Him in His talk" (v. 15). The response of Jesus suggests that the stimulus of trickery would try divine patience.

[4] James 1:2. *Peirasmaos* is used in this verse as "trials," varied and assorted. The Greek word for *"various"* implies several kinds; *poikilos* is used of strange doctrines in Hebrews 13:9. Such false doctrines are both foreign to the gospel and they are, like trials, diversified.

[5] Lawrence O. Richards, *Expository Dictionary of Bible Words* (Grand Rapids, MI: The Zondervan Corp., 1985), 593.

[6] *The MacArthur Study Bible.* editor John MacArthur (Nashville, TE: Thomas Nelson Co., 1997), 1883.

[7] Romans 14:23. See note 8, chapter 3.

[8] James 1:13. Not that God does not enlist evil agents (or good agents that rouse evil) for His ultimate good purpose and glory (Job 1:12; 2 Ch 18:19–22), but the Scripture here carefully teaches that God is not involved in the actual succoring or the solicitation to do evil. His decree is always redemptive toward humanity, yet it does secure the evil as well as the good to accomplish His righteous ends.

[9] James 1:14. Inner depravity is said to be the true culprit behind transgression, especially of all Adam's posterity (Rom 5:12). As our verse conveys, one is "drawn away by his own lusts and desires," leaving the accountability for transgression squarely upon one's own choice.

[10] Luke 22:31. The insight from the Lord would suggest to Peter that Satan himself was continually at Peter's heels to waste him. The next verse, however, discloses that Peter was well able to resist devilish inroads

through faith in Christ. The promise of intercession from the Savior would be of great consolation and encouragement to Peter amid intense warfare, just as it should be for all those who rely upon God (v. 32).

11 Second Corinthians 10:3–6. Here is a good passage on the nature of the battle for the mind. The warfare is said to be a spiritual one, as opposed to one that is waged in the flesh. In practical terms, mere methodology or human therapy can never accomplish in the mind what spiritual means is able to resolve. Short term fixes, displaced idolatries, and psychological bandages are the best things that can be done for the life that employs nominal means of combat. Mastery over fear is anticipated by the soldier who makes use of God's arsenal. Struggle, combat, and fighting are always a part of life in the Spirit, but the divine strategy of obedient thinking is powerful through God to the overthrow of strongholds.

12 James 4:7. The immediate context deals with barring Satan's inroads from one's heart and mind by all humility (v. 6). Implicit to humility is submission to God, versus resistance in the flesh, which is pride. The Devil's swift exit is promised where deference to God is acted upon.

13 Romans 6:14. This is a verse that cannot be overstated. See note 2, chapter 3.

14 Matthew 8:26. Matthew's account of the Galilee wind storm: same event, different narrator. The evident lesson of faith makes its mark upon the disciple recording this frightful experience.

15 Acts 2. The church is born upon the descent of the Holy Spirit. Pentecost ignites the frazzled followers of the Lamb to answer reveille and turn their world upside down with the gospel of Jesus Christ. The book of Acts might better be titled "The Acts of the Holy Spirit."

16 Romans 8:29. The lesson of the apostle Paul is to educate his believing audience with the truth that conformity to the moral excellence of Jesus Christ is the destination of all believers. All those whom God holds in His loving favor from eternity past, He purposed to conform (Gk. *summorphizo*), or "to make them in to the form" of Christ Himself, the exalted Brother. Tenacity amid life's tumult is symptomatic of God's effectual purpose. See also Phlp 1:6 and 2:12, 13; 1 Th 5:23, 24; and Rom 8:29 in its context.

[17] First Peter 5:7–9. Although persecution is implied by the use of the word "sufferings" in v. 9, Peter's first epistle gives a much broader application to the word. Included in the broader scope of the letter is the believer's suffering in his daily struggle with the flesh (1 Pe 4:1, 2). As Christ was crucified for sin, true saints should "arm themselves with the same mind," that is, to "crucify the flesh with its passions and desires" (Ga 5:24). Whatever else may be implied by the suffering addressed in 1 Peter 4:1, 2, the crucifixion of the flesh is conveyed, and one surely suffers, but in a liberating way (see Mt 5:29, 30).

[18] First Peter 4:16. Peter admonishes Christians to suffer for a righteous cause, rather than unrighteous character. The manner of suffering among Christians should reflect the glory of God first and above all self-serving motivation. Logic would underscore this application to the whole realm of human suffering as blood-bought offspring of Jesus. In other words, what part of the human experience of suffering might exempt ransomed sons from bringing glory to God?

[19] Philippians 4:9. See note 7, chapter 2.

[20] Philippians 2:12, 13. What a comfort throughout the storm of life. "You work out your salvation with fear and trembling," Paul admonishes. However, what follows bolsters our courage like the strength of an ocean current sweeping us forward, for God is at work in you, both willing and doing His good pleasure. Work. Work it out. Maintain a work mentality in your faith, Paul teaches—knowing full well that God Himself is inciting and sustaining all forward motion. We must always remember how these verses, once again, presume divine sovereignty and human responsibility.

[21] Philippians 3:12–15. The apostle Paul viewed life as an Olympic event where runners endure great hardship to seize the prize. The upward call of God in Christ Jesus (v. 14) was the purpose and end of Paul's earthly course of discipline, rigor, and hardship. He was willing to endure every obstacle, every hurdle, in order to obtain his objective in grace. The passage before us paints a vivid portrait of the mind-set characteristic of the Christian competitor, the apostle himself being the model that divine inspiration accentuates.

22 Second Timothy 4:4–8. Once again, the mind-set of mastery over every obstacle is Paul's example and admonition for young Pastor Timothy. "Endure afflictions," Paul urges upon Timothy. The apostle Paul anticipates his death (v. 6) while reflecting upon the good fight and the great race (v. 7). Here, the thought finishes with the personal disclosure of a coming reward for himself and for all those who "have loved His appearing." The tense of the word "loved" (v. 8) suggests that attitude of heart that propelled faith's contestant throughout his battle with the world, the flesh, and the Devil.

23 Psalm 46:1. The reader should note the lyric and lines that follow such a blessed boon: "Therefore, we will not fear, even though the earth be removed, and the mountains be carried in the midst of the sea; though its waters roar and be troubled, though the mountains shake with its swelling" (vv. 2, 3). Now, what could be more disconcerting to the mind than the physical implosion of our physical world and the oceans unleashed by the might of a tsunami? The point is, nothing can rival the help almighty God provides to all those who truly rely upon the refuge and strength of His Person.

24 Job 19:25. Out of the oldest canonical book, Job gives early testament to his experienced knowledge of the true and living God. The ascription "Redeemer" preceded by the pronoun "my" tells us of the saving nature of Job's relationship with the Almighty. This personal union was the basis for his hope in future resurrection and the continued conscious reality of beholding God in truth and in immortal union and joy. See verses 26, 27.

25 Psalm 19:7. The nature of God's Word, God's statutes, God's Law is said to convert (i.e., change, transform, regenerate) the soul. So, at the seat of human behavior, God's Word is well able to change a person thoroughly, from the inside out. The testimony of human experience over the millennia attests to this reality.

26 First Peter 1:13. I've given this parallel rendering from the Greek text in order to further benefit the reader's understanding of this verse: "In your thinking, gather up all that is not tied down; be morally collective with accomplished hope in the grace being brought to you at the revelation of Jesus Christ."

CHAPTER 5

Sticks, Slingshots, and Other Proven Methods

> So the Philistine said to David, "Am I a dog that you come to me with sticks?" And the Philistine cursed David by his gods. (Sam. 17:43)

We know David had his shepherd's staff in his hand, together with his sling, as he drew near Goliath (1 Sam 17:40).[1] The term "sticks," as rendered in the English version, suggests disdain, disgust, and ridicule on the Philistine's part, especially when Goliath erupted with the words, "Am I a dog?" (1 Sam 17:43).[2] He might have more accurately said, "Am I a sheep, that you come to me with a shepherd's staff?" Ah, but Goliath is unconcerned with any specific description; he was out to bring fear to his adversary by trash talk (see 1 Sam 17:44).[3]

Philosophy of Methodology

The point of our discussion, however, is sticks and slingshots. You see, David used means, and God evidently blessed their usage! David used them to protect his father's flock in the wilderness. God obviously blessed them in that place and in David's hand, just as God used them mightily with the defeat of the Philistine champion.

In fact, the God of Israel blessed the fine-tuned army of King David with much skill in the use of weaponry.

Have you ever walked through the directory of King David's mighty men of valor? Actually, there's a good deal of Scripture concerning them and the particular skills and accomplishments of these very special warriors. A good place to review what God has said about them is 1 Chronicles, chapter 11. Here, we have a sizeable list, but we'll simply focus in on a few. Well, there was:

Benaiah, the son of Jehoida, killed an Egyptian over seven feet in height. The Egyptian had a very large spear, like that of a "weaver's beam," which Benaiah wrestled out of the warrior's own hand, killing him with it. Look carefully to what was in Benaiah's hand and was used with great skill to snag this large man's spear: a staff, a shepherd's staff (v. 23).[4] There are several terms in the Hebrew language that could be represented by the English word "staff," but a shepherd's staff would best characterize the word used here.

The shepherd's staff could be used for blunt trauma, such as warding off predatory persons or animals. It could be quickly altered to rescue a lamb by its crook end, perhaps from the mouth of a wild bear, or to lift a sheep from a crevice or rock ledge. Such practice and expertise in the use of the staff could be formidable on the battlefront, especially in snagging the adversary's weapon from out of his hand. Swift beatings, poking jabs, swinging distraction, and then—snag! Your weapon is plucked out of your hand! The rest is history (yes, God blessed Benaiah's skill, together with his staff).

Then, there was Abishai, who "lifted up his spear against 300 men, killed them, and won a name ..." (v. 20).[5] Now, biblical words need careful attention so that the reader doesn't miss the bounty that inspiration affords. The words "lifted up" here imply so much more than what meets the eye. The practiced, skillful way Abishai wielded and threw the spear can only be explained as a phenomenon, as extraordinary, or the quality of experience that appears almost unreal, yet it is true.

HARNESSING THE HARASSMENT OF HUMAN FEARS

Personally, and in contention with several world class athletes, I have met some wrestlers who were simply phenomenal. It's as if their skills went beyond the range of my capabilities. I remember talking to the teammate of a certain wrestler who had showed me the lights early and efficiently. Inquiring about his abilities and still trying to figure out what had just happened to me, my opponent's teammate replied, "Don't worry about it; he's just very bright. He wrestles like his IQ."

So what did that say about me? The fact of the matter was, my competitor had read me earlier, had baited the way for my demise, and had used even my aggression against me—with an exclamation point! Where I had thought three moves ahead, he had been thinking a series of counters and maneuvers that seemed creative and customized. Smarts was a good part of it, but showing that sort of skill and conditioning takes precision practicing, over and over again. Now, think with me. Add that sort of elitism with the Spirit of the living God, and you'll need to trust your running skills when you are on deck to face a warrior like Abishai.

Other great accounts include Eleazor, who stood his ground on the battlefield and took out so many Philistines that the day went to Israel. Eleazor was credited with Israel's rout (v. 14).[6] You've got to read of Jashobeam—with a name like that, you have to wonder what he might be hurling at his enemy in battle (v. 11).[7]

Besides the long list of David's mighty warriors, there are other groups of men who are honored for their extraordinary skills, like those who came to David at Ziklag in 1 Chronicles 12, "armed with bows, using both the right hand and the left in hurling stones and shooting arrows with the bow" (v. 2).[8]

Now, what does all this have to do with imparting a philosophy of methodology? My answer to the inquiry is this: these are but a few illustrations among many that would teach us that the Lord of all has purposed means in the defense of His people! Faith does not negate effort or good sense in the employment of legitimate means to assist us in the spiritual fray. God never reproved Israel for the use of military means; He only decries our trust in these as the singular avenue of success.

The triumphs of David's army had much to do with the expertise and the skill of his men, but we must never forget those little, tucked-away portions of the text that indicate to us who truly was behind the men and their means. First Chronicles 12:18[9] declares, "Then the Spirit came upon Amasai, chief of the captains, and he said, 'We are yours, O David; we are on your side, O son of Jessie! Peace, peace to you, and peace to your helpers. For your God helps you!' So, David received them, and made them captains of the troop."

The sons of Benjamin and Judah discerned rightly that the living God enabled David and his military might. Obviously, the Spirit of God enabled these brethren to strengthen David's hand, because David would not have given Amasai and his colleagues the stature of captains, unless both their character and their skills were tantamount.

As we have said before, the struggle for a sound mind in a broken world is warfare—spiritual warfare (Eph 6:10–12).[10]

Interestingly, the Devil is said to use wiles! Now, what in the world does the term *wiles* mean? Webster's Dictionary would lend this understanding: "A sly trick; deceitful artifice; stratagem."[11] But the best description is the one that comes closest to the Greek word itself. *Method* is the word; Ephesians 6:11 is the text and, yes, the root term *method* is exactly what wiles looks like. The Devil (and his associates) uses methods, *hodos* (i.e., ways and means). He is very cunning in his craft and he knows how to play up irrational fears in the hearts and minds of those he targets.

Conversely, God sanctions means, and one must make use of all legitimate biblically sanctioned and sifted methods. I believe God delights in creative, ambitious, and strategizing warriors who battle the world, the flesh, and the Devil with rigor and ruthlessness! Practiced counter habits (Eph 4:22–24),[12] thought switchage (1 Cor 9:24)[13] and stoppage (Rom 6:11),[14] support (1 Th 5:11),[15] reassurance (1

John 3:18, 19),[16] modeling (John 13:14),[17] assertiveness (Titus 2:15),[18] and any other technique that does not violate biblical principles or distract from the person of Jesus Christ is fair game.

However, we must underscore this truth: methods, in themselves, don't make people like Christ (Ps 33:16–22).[19] Ultimate deliverance that will harness fear and spring the soul upward into the image of God is not found in crafted weaponry, but in the Savior, by His own Spirit, through His Word! If these are not the grounds for all enablement, then our success is vain, our techniques are shallow, and our remedy is but a placebo (Ps 44:4–8;[20] Prov 21:31).[21]

Methods can be very helpful, but there is far more to the conflict in which we are engaged than mere results. True believers are, first and foremost, concerned for the glory of God. Therefore, they are free to use only those strategies that honor Him. Our Redeemer is concerned with the whole picture of the good fight. Our Redeemer is concerned with the technician, and He is concerned with his technique as telltale to the nature of his confidence (1 Sam 17:47).[22]

Mind Benders and Mood-Altering Meds

A number of years ago, I had the opportunity to mentor a physician who was a friend and brother in the gospel. In the course of our discussions about the use of psychotropic drugs, my good friend shared with me a story I will not soon forget.

Among his several responsibilities as a physician was the task of being the official doctor for a local public school. Apparently, there were some serious discipline problems, especially among students in the fifth grade. The problems were widespread in that grade, bringing together school officials with this physician to brainstorm solutions.

According to my friend, an off-the-record conversation ensued, which precipitated an inquiry of the doctor something like this: "Doctor, what would be your thoughts of putting our fifth graders on Ritalin?"

The question was not asked in a humorous tone, but in candid honesty as a possible solution to a solemn, student management issue. Well, thankfully, the good doctor took that idea off the table! This school board member suggested the all-too-common quick fix for a moral issue dilemma: take a drug!

Ritalin would certainly put an immediate Band-Aid on the hard-to-manage classroom. Methylphenidate (Ritalin) is a prescription for minimal brain dysfunction in children, according to the medical world. It targets social, educational, and psychological disorders, among other problems. So if you're dealing with distraction in your classroom, emotional instability among the students, impulsive, hyperactive children—could Ritalin be the answer?

In fact, I have personally observed the effects of the drug upon preteen boys in the setting of an elementary school classroom. The once flamboyant, colorful personalities of these preadolescent, mischievous boys were completely changed. Their moods took on a more subdued and solemn appearance in contrast to the jocular disposition of active boys (yes, too active sometimes for their britches). The parents, however, prescribed the change through the use of Ritalin.

I would agree that such children are more manageable, but, in my observation, something is terribly wrong. Sacrificial nurturing had been replaced by a quick fix. Parental perseverance to careful involvement, structure, and love—over time—nurtures "personalism."

Now, let me define personalism. It is the individual expression of those Creator-endowed qualities intended to impress and impact others. Would you not agree that the strategies we employ for the management of our flesh should express our personhood, our being?

Granted, several areas would need to be addressed regarding the young people in our two accounts: much parental sacrifice, the careful reassessment of priorities, evaluation of values, structured and spontaneous involvement, the awareness for parental example and change, together with the intentional cooperation of school personnel. The point is, nurturing the identity of personhood takes effort. God is in the business of developing His people into mature people, and this He does quite intimately as well as over time. In cases such as these, God's purposes seem to contradict the use of a central nervous system stimulant. With that said, God also has a reputation for working in lives, despite our diagnostic missteps.

Human nature just has a way of avoiding personal culpability. It's always easier to excuse our behaviors than to take ownership for our sins. Adam's posterity has a proclivity for sidestepping responsibility for these attitudes and actions, so psychological labels have become the craze. Sadly, all too often the diagnosis is another complicating misstep, dwarfing both the wisdom and maturity of *being*.

Now, how about meds and irrational fears in specific? I have refused them! I want a rational conflict against unreasonable thinking. I choose the clear-minded approach while thrusting myself before God, in faith, resisting all foreign aid.

Please remember that my subject has to do with irrational fear, this whole area of bizarre or out-of-control thinking resultant from caving in to threatening stimuli. I am talking about that which 2 Timothy 1:7[23] discerns as not given us by God.

Again, this fear is the opposite of soundness, which term innately lends the idea of discipline and/or self-control, or yet, "saving the mind." Furthermore, the verse states a truth and a fact—even a promise of faith for all those who lean hard upon its application. Obviously, the lesson at hand is to awaken God's people to the reality of the lordship of Christ over our bodies, and that certainly includes our minds.

Mental soundness is as much our God's business as is our spiritual fitness (2 Tim 1:7).[24] The impact of God's Word upon our total lives results in radical change with the permanent effects of peace, joy, love, hope, and righteousness. When used in the skillful hands of godly pastors, teachers, and counselors, the Bible becomes the most effective tool to solve problems at their source. Thank God for sound medical advice, but thank the Lord for the resource of biblical truth that is able to "divide joints and marrow" and "discern thoughts and intents"[25] of the heart!

Naturally, the question is asked, "What about those who come for counseling who are already using psychotropic treatment as prescribed by their doctors?"

Good question. Well, I counsel such individuals where they are and work with their doctors, as much as possible. My objective is getting these folks to sit, walk, and stand—without their drugs or dependencies, especially if they are brethren. You see, my goal as a servant of Christ is to support, assist, and cultivate the sanctifying process. The process, of course, is the apprehension of Christ's all-sufficiency, just as Psalm 23:1 declares, "The Lord is my Shepherd, I shall not want," or this: "I have all that I need, because the Lord is my shepherd." This text corresponds well with what Paul is teaching in Colossians 2:9, 10,[26] "For in Him [Jesus Christ], dwells all the fullness of the Godhead bodily, and you are complete in Him, who is the head of all principality and power."

These verses are potent! They are so full of rich wonder, theologically, while the practical gain, when engrafted into the mind and heart, is liberating, to say the least! It is vital to get folks thinking critically about their minds and about their hearts in this passing pilgrimage.

Unreality of faith must be the most wasting disease of Christianity today. Drug marketing is a huge business in the psychotropic field alone. Sadly, my research tells me that addiction, side effects, and other relative information about such drugs are not fully understood by medical science, while most prescribing physicians have little knowledge and training in the area of psychopharmacology.

Millions of people, including a startling, growing number of Christians, turn their minds over to the "experts" with little investigation or reserve. Perhaps a more radical approach is needed from our pulpits today to restore confidence in both the authority and sufficiency of God's truth among His people. "The statutes of the Lord are right, rejoicing the heart; the commandment of the Lord is pure, enlightening the eyes ..." (Ps 19:8).[27]

In specific, thoroughly biblical advice concerning drug use for irrational fears should be discussed openly with those who come for counsel or look to us for help. The discussion should be forthright, non-judgmental, but always redemptive. Herein is trusted counsel for the whole mind and the heart made whole.

Let me carefully follow up this section of our study by sharing some matters of pertinent consideration. The psychotropic include the whole gamut of drugs from cocaine to alcohol, heroin to caffeine, as well as mind-affecting drugs prescribed by physicians and psychiatrists.

Antidepressants and sedative-hypnotic related drugs fall under this psychotropic category in the treatment of anxiety. These are all drugs that alter a certain aspect of consciousness. Let me advise caution at this point. Before using any of these medications, counsel with your pastor. He may refer you to a sound biblical counselor. Whether you are considering taking such drugs or desiring to reduce your medication, ask your physician to help you slowly come off the med. Stopping psychotropic medication "cold turkey" could be very harmful to your health and well being.

Even where the usage of these meds are deemed necessary and legitimate (1 Tim 5:23;[28] Prov 31:4–7),[29] prayer and caution are givens.

I think the question to be asked in any situation where psychotropic treatment is urged is whether or not viable physiological issues are evident. When you're given a clean bill of health but the doctor insists upon Lorazepam for anxious moments, an alarm should go off in your head.

It is true that learned Bible teachers and biblical counselors are not physicians, but on the other hand, most physicians speak from a purely secular medical model. Be suspect in such cases and do not allow yourself to throw caution to the wind. Think biblically! Think in healing ways! Contemplate the mind of Christ!

Several years ago, I faced my first major surgery experience. The many years of head spinning, neck bridging, and shoulder rolls had taken their toll. My neck was my vulnerable area. It was that part of my upper body that sustained the serious injuries in my wrestling career.

Still coaching and wrestling with the guys and doing head spins at age fifty-seven, well, one night it happened. A slight pain went through my back. The pain was enough to jolt my thinking and cause me to wonder, so I backed away, took a shower, and went home to what would be the beginning of serious physical agony.

Honestly and without exaggeration, it was the worst pain I have experienced in my life. Unable to sleep lying on my back or on either side, I tried slumping over the living room hassock while my beloved wife prayed for my relief and rest. I even tried catching sleep like horses and cows: standing up. It didn't work, and it doesn't work!

I went to a notable therapist/trainer who administered a traction-type apparatus that stretched out my neck, and the mechanism operated on a timer. Talk about stimulus for fear! The neck is clamped, the neck is stretching, the timer is set, and the therapist leaves, closing the door behind him. Isn't life grand? Boy, did I pray, praise, and repent! "Lord," I said, "I will never again do foolish antics like this; no more wrestling."

Seems like I should have gotten the message earlier when I would crawl into the house, bruised and bleeding, and my dearest would say, "I'm not going to ask you why you do this to yourself." Well, there I was, and now the doctors had me on Oxycodone, a drug with a real issue of addiction as a side effect.

Finally, the day drew near when the extensive picture-taking of my neck—pictures from every possible angle using all the latest cinematography, so it seemed—was over. I can play it all today on my large-screen with the DVD they "gifted" me. (Someday,

I'll write a sequel on those dreaded, claustro-cameras. You know, the type where the living are electronically conveyed into a burial chamber to then hear a voice saying, "don't breathe—breathe—stop breathing." Oh, wow. Thank God for His enabling!)

Pictures in hand, the doctors had all conspired, uh, I mean, conferred and decided that surgery was necessary. Two discs had herniated, another was severely compressed, and all needed reconstruction and fusion with a metal plate—among other things.

Convinced "the thing was of the Lord," I consented to a procedure that was yet two months out. The searing pain was still there, made tolerable by the medication, but perspiration yet rolled down my face while I preached every Sunday morning. I certainly had an audience that was attendant to my words in those suffering days.

Then, in my last office visit with my regular physician, he popped a question: "Do you have suicidal thoughts?" Wait a minute; my doctor knew me. He had collected the data for years. I was not quiet about my hope, my world view, my confidence in life. Yet he asked of me an honest question to which I replied, "Doc, I have absolute confidence in my God. No, I have no suicidal thoughts." "That's good," he replied. "I was concerned about your state of mind due to pain and sleeplessness."

There they were: viable physiological issues. I was emitting some jittery emotion, some flux of reason, yea, some anxiety exacerbated by somatic issues. He saw it, and I knew it, and to shorten the story, a few days before the operation, I took two out of the six Lorazepam tablets that I was prescribed, 0.5 milligrams per tablet. This prescription targeted the aggravated anxiety.

Surgery went well. Apart from a tingling residue in my left hand, the pain is gone. I am back to crazy workouts, but no more mat stuff; that's for the younger guys. It's time for grandchildren and scrapbooks and an occasional loving comment from my wife regarding those slimmer photographs.

Earlier, I said that I refuse any psychotropic and that I do so in the quest for a sound mind. Where legitimate physiological or somatic issues exist, discernment is needed.

In special cases, similar to the situation afore mentioned, I have counseled clients to continue usage while marinating their hearts with Christ's all-sufficiency and immersing their minds with Christ's absolute right of influence (Eph 5:18).[30]

Need we say it again? The irrational fears of an otherwise healthy person provide an opportunity for maturity through warfare: Mercenary help—foreign aid— is the easy way out of a venturous faith. Influences that circumvent the Holy Spirit in the progress of sanctification must be discarded as spiritual inhibitors, even though they spell r-e-l-i-e-f.

About Those Proven Means

The last chapter of this book has been reserved for rehab samples, resources that have helped me personally, and practical applications relative to fighting fear. In this brief segment, my intention is to assist those who struggle by offering a little organization, a little planning, and a bit of "how to" for the actual engagement with fear.

It has been my sincere desire to provide concepts of truth and doable insights that have enabled me and others to exercise mastery over fearful thinking. In this sense, what is being shared comes out of a life context, as opposed to pure theory. No one can claim originality for the finds of this book, however, since what we know and experience in the truth comes to us from God. Truth, then, is ours for discovery and the acquisition of wisdom is seen through the restatement of truth in the way we live.

The trusted, tried and proven counsel of God's Word awaits to be exposited in a life context and when it is, the yield is sufficient for "all things that pertain to life and godliness" (2 Pe 1:3).[31]

In the contemplation of my next bout with the stimulus for fear, whenever and wherever, these things I plan, I strategize:

First: Express yourself. Self-talk with the goal to restore reason (1 Tim 4:16).[32]

One thing that is very much a part of your and my identity as human beings is self-awareness. *I think, therefore, I am.*[33] Every day when I awaken, I am aware of myself. Even when I sleep and dream, I am aware of myself in the context of my dream world. Even though we may not verbalize our self-talk, we humans are always talking to ourselves inwardly: reflecting, calculating, conferencing, deciding, and planning.

Counseling ourselves is a good thing, especially when we are giving ourselves sound advice. "Take heed to yourself," Paul admonishes, "and to the doctrine." In fact, 1 Timothy 4:16 tells us to continue doing this for the deliverance of yourself and for the deliverance of those to whom you minister. Wow! What a plan: self-talk about the teaching.

Take heed, Mark, I have said to myself, *Your Redeemer is strong. He will make a way of escape. Embrace it, engage it.* Now, there are many more things in the realm of sound counsel that I have given myself, but let me suggest that you devise several short, confrontational-type scenarios for yourself as you engage the "event." It will become necessary to speak the truth aloud sometimes. We live in the Bluetooth era, so many people who may be around or close by you might simply think you're talking on the cell; just get beyond self-awareness and speak in challenging tones to your heart and mind. Check out more samples in chapter seven of this book.

Let me encourage the reader to write out several scenarios, as I have suggested, ahead of time. Plan your counseling session well. Keep it short and directed; most importantly, listen. Take heed to your own counsel! Think on your words. Prove the biblicality of the wisdom that you are sharing with yourself by focusing on the sense and meaning of the words you are hearing. Restore reason by deflecting your thoughts to another fixation, even a fixation with the truth. One further note: for emphasis, keep your counsel substantive, but brief. When the alarm sounds, the swift execution of your plan is essential. After all, this is warfare!

Second: Employ your strategy. Use ways and means (1 Sam 17:40).[34]

A fear episode escalates so rapidly that those who struggle will often remark that it simply overwhelmed them, taking them by surprise. In many cases, people have expressed their seeming inability to focus, or think. They were simply blindsided.

I can completely identify with such a scene. One of the worst instances in my experience with claustrophobic encounters came several years back in the dead of winter. It was a very cold day in central New York; the temperature hovered near zero or below. I was leaving my church office for an errand and jumped into my car. I'm not sure why the remote enabled me to get in, because once the car locked, all doors froze up and would not let me out. Boom! The windows were iced, the car was cold, and I was alone in a fairly large parking lot.

Of course, without a moment's notice, my mind and body told me that I needed to get out of the car. Like now. No time to warm things up; I was physically prepared to get out—feet first, straight through the side window.

Believe me, if I had continued thinking that way for a few moments longer, I would have emerged, bloodied, if need be, but free at last! Hallelujah, grace ensued as I lifted an emotional *Help!* to God and focused rapidly on the remote button, intending to speed dial my local mechanic, pronto!

The idea, here, is multitasking. It keeps you from fixing your thoughts on the fear feeling. You might ask me, "How were you in any condition to talk to your mechanic without sounding stupid crazy?" That's the point. The situation would force me to communicate rationally and catch my breath. I have used the telephone method before—intentional conversation with a person in close proximity. This helps send the scare in a remedial direction.

Now, then, somewhere in the fray, the lock mechanism responded to my fervent demands, and I was able to talk to my mechanic on the downside of things. He explained what had happened while I settled into a calming pattern and contemplated how to resolve freeze-ups in the future.

Engage the event by employing your strategy. Seek weaponry that will bring the episode down to reality. Do this, both in the conflict as well as after the fact. Recall the scene as it *really* is and size down irrational, larger-than-life mental images.

If I must use elevators, and most pastors must for hospital visitation, I plan for the ride. Reading is essential for me in the climb or the descent. I will read Scripture or an article, and sometimes I have purposed to rearrange my wallet, perusing important data that I need to remember. I have upgraded my use of the cell phone at such times, intentionally using the elevator as an opportunity to get more technically efficient. You get the idea!

Plan concretes, doables, strategies, weapons, methods, and all legitimate means to subdue the threat. Further helps are just ahead in our reading, but the thrust here is choose your methods. Find what is most helpful to you on the battlefield. Log it. Record it. Engraft the strategy, and with vigilance look to the next event where you may use it with expertise and for the glory of the Lord!

Third: Evaluate strong defenses. Cultivate courage from past victories (2 Tim 4:7).[35]

There is a certain maturity and confidence that experience and accomplishment afford. The more notches on your belt, the more lift to your step as you square off with the adversary. Hebrews 5:14 is a stellar text to use here. In essence, the verse teaches that maturity (i.e., "full age") belongs to those who are skilled in the use of solid food, or Bible truth. In fact, these mature ones have come of age due to exercise, applying truth to discern right and wrong. This they have done again and again, until they have obtained a high level of skill and proficiency.

Now, most of us have asked while studying the Old Testament, why Israel doubted the Lord just after His parting of the Red Sea. I mean, time after time, there were mighty deliverances by an awesome God and, yet, we hear, "We want to go back to Egypt, to bondage."[36]

Too often, this was the response of God's people. You would think the multiple experiences of Yahweh's might and power would have given the children of Israel an unstoppable perspective. Mind renewal is the needful art of courageous soldiers (Rom 12:2)[37] The continual recall of divine enablement and past deliverance is essential to future successes on the battlefront.

Habitually recall those savory times when things appeared intolerable, even impossible, and then, out you went, straight through the fight by the high hand of God. Reflect on those times *often* in praise.

Recall the events with thanksgiving in prayer. Return to the scenes in your mind and use them for witness and testimony to others, but get them down with paper and ink.

Confidence in the Captain is bottom line for a strong defense against the next onslaught. He has delivered you in the past, and He will deliver you again. Experience assures this and promise confirms this; you will return home with His joy in your heart. Yes, the testing will be for a season of time, but it certainly yields peaceable fruits to those who stay close to the King (1 Pe 1:6, 7).[38]

What questions might we ask of ourselves, in reflection, to help us in all future skirmishes? Meditate on the following data:

1. What was the situation? In other words, paint again the scene of conflict that gave rise to the temptation of irrational thinking. Just google up the situation in your mind's eye, but don't give too much attention to the feel of fear.

2. What were the odds? Measure up all that was against you. For example: *I was tempted to lose it, to run from my*

responsibility, to hide, to shrink into a box. I was fearful about hurting myself and others. I contemplated defeat. Then, measure up all that was *for* you. For example, *I believe El-Elyon* [the strongest strong one] *was present. I spoke His promise to my heart with a faith cry for help. I used His proven weaponry* (i.e., thought distraction, assertive witness, enlisted prayer support, the immediate accountability of one's mate, etc.). There was more going for me than against me—by far!

3. What was the outcome? Get expressive! Whoop it up in your mind: *The devil got his fingers slammed pulling at the latch-string of my heart. He fled. This was a good fight where God showed Himself mighty on my behalf. I remember having a "bring it on mentality." This battle strengthened me in the following ways …,* etc.

4. What lesson(s) have I tucked into my heart as I recall this strong defense, either in my walk with God or in my choice of means? What have I learned? What worked best? In whom do I hope? Then, add all of this data to your diary, or wherever you log your insights, as part of your ready recall.

So there we have it: some organization for our madness. Much, much more information could be expressed, but this should give us direction, provide some help, and incite further ideas and creative industry. Like the joy in your heart when the answer of your mouth reflects the wisdom of God (Prov 15:23)[39], so there is something rewarding to the soul when your thoughtful planning comes to fruition. May God prosper you in this endeavor!

Chapter Five Footnotes

[1] First Samuel 17:40. We may assume David's staff and sling were in opposite hands. Surely, the young man appeared as a common shepherd as he approached the veteran warrior, Goliath. The giant failed to consider, however, that the ruddy youth dressed in unpretentious garb was quite lethal in the hands of Almighty God.

[2] First Samuel 17:43. The verse documents the vile outbursts of a pagan warrior. Intimidation and fear was the intention of Goliath. The gods of the Philistines were many, Dagon being the most revered. Dagon appeared as half man and half fish. It is the idol that Jehovah decimated before the Ark of the Covenant in the house of Dagon (1 Sam 5:1–5).

[3] First Samuel 17:44. The cursing of the Philistine led to more graphic threats of annihilation. The verbal disdain from Goliath suggested that David would become bird food and animal chow. David's retort was similar, only the young man's words were prophetic (v. 46).

[4] First Chronicles 11:23. It might be well to note that a weaver's beam measured approximately two to two and a half inches in diameter, so the Egyptian's spear was comparable to Goliath's own weapon (1 Sam 17:7).

[5] First Chronicles 11:20. Abishai won a name for himself; however, Abishai distinguishes himself as more honorable than the other two men (v. 21).

[6] First Chronicles 11:14. The verse says "they," or the three mighty men, stationed themselves in the midst of the field and prevailed against the Philistines. It should be noted, however, that only Eleazor's name is mentioned here, and he seems most prominent in the outcome of the battle (vv. 12–14).

[7] First Chronicles 11:11. On one occasion, it is said that Jashobeam killed three hundred men with the spear at one time, while 2 Samuel 23:8 cites eight hundred men. Whether a copyist error in the tally or otherwise, the feat is enormous.

8 First Chronicles 12:2. The versatility of David's warriors is evident in the description where these men could both use the bow and hurl stones, right-handed or left-handed, with expertise. Truly, these men were an "army of one."

9 First Chronicles 12:18. The point I wish to assert is the fact that God's own Spirit declares through the mouth of Amasai that David is assisted in his military ventures by God Himself. Clearly, God helped David's helpers (soldiers).

10 Ephesians 6:10–12. Paul is not simply drawing an analogy of the Christian life and comparing it to the earthly struggle of combat among warring peoples, but He is declaring that, in all reality, the Christian life itself is a battle with unseen evil forces. Though the nature of the conflict is not identical and the weaponry differs in type, the onslaught is very real and the adversary is very much alive! The hostile force is organized and functions with strategy. Success for the Christian must, of course, be tied to the Lord as we wage warfare in the power He promises to provide His troops.

11 *Webster New World Dictionary, Second College Edition*, ed. in chief, David B. Guralnik (New York: Prentice Hall Press, 1984).

12 Ephesians 4:22–24. Not unlike the behaviorist technique of practicing a remedial habit in place of a debilitating one, the apostle teaches putting off the old and putting on the new. Although the motivation for change is radically different for the believer as opposed to the humanist, people are, nonetheless, creatures of habit. God knows this and has designed the process of habituation as a viable law of change.

13 First Corinthians 9:24. Here is an illustration for the technique known as "thought switchage," where Paul sees life's pilgrimage, with all of its labors, hardships, disciplines, and service, as a race where runners exhaust themselves to lay hold of the prize. Imagining himself an Olympian, the apostle Paul embraces life with visions of the rigors of training, the arena, the prize to be won. Switching his thoughts in this manner appears to motivate this gospel servant to color his perspective of life, enabling maximum output as he looks to life's challenges through a variety of

lenses—i.e., wrestling (Eph 6:12); boxing (1 Cor 9:26); and marathon running (Heb 12:1).

14 Romans 6:11. Thought stoppage could be employed in the curtailing of sin by reckoning with the death of self. This method, used in a doctrinal framework by the embattled Christian, puts a stop to our carnal way of thinking or acting as one resigns to the crucifixion of self. The cross curtails the encroachments of evil when mental posturing becomes real and radical!

15 First Thessalonians 5:11. Comfort and support are the means of edification. In particular, as we comfort, we are using divine strategy to help others (and ourselves) recover to spiritual strength and stability. Again, biblical support differs from mere behaviorist support in the direction it serves (i.e., the glory of God).

16 First John 3:18, 19. John would reassure his readers concerning their union with God by the fact of their active love for others. The Holy Spirit Himself uses reassurance from a fellow warrior as the means to encourage holy resolve in the lives of God's own.

17 John 13:14. Modeling is a strong tool for change in the Christian, as well as in the non-Christian counseling circles. The principle of modeling behavior as a way of conveying a lesson and influencing change is used by our Lord as He washed the disciples' feet, "Do as I have done to you," Jesus said. Thus, modeling becomes a legitimate strategy, a biblical game tactic for character enhancement.

18 Titus 2:15. Titus had great responsibility as he set in order the "things that were lacking" in all the Cretan churches (1:5). Paul, therefore, admonishes assertiveness in the task. Titus was to engage his labor and his audience with the force of resolve, or confidence. The technique is viable, one in which Paul himself was exercised and skilled.

19 Psalm 33:16–22. These verses are beautiful lines of meditation rehearsing the truth that all victory comes to us through God's enablement alone. The army doesn't save the King (v. 16a), but God uses armies to bring deliverance. A mighty man does not prevail because of his great strength (v. 16b), something Samson learned the hard way. However, God does use

HARNESSING THE HARASSMENT OF HUMAN FEARS

a man's strength to subdue his rival. A horse is a vain thing in which to hope (v. 17), but alas, Solomon was fortified by a vast cavalry under the providential hand of the Almighty. The passage finds application to all the "ways and means" of personal deliverance and spiritual progress. Unless the Lord is trusted, all the prowess and skill of ingenious methodology will fail to liberate the human heart at the core of its need.

[20] Psalm 44:4–8. The lyric vents the anthem of souls set free, even "In God we boast all day long" (v. 8). Here is the source of our perfecting, for the truth lies in this everlasting axiom, "You are my King, O God. Command victories for Jacob" (v. 4).

[21] Proverbs 21:31. What a profound sentence from Solomon; if only he had sought its remedy when he entertained the company of strange and idolatrous women. If Solomon thought his clever sense would deliver him, then his own cunning failed him as he laid aside the spirit of this proverb.

[22] Second Samuel 17:47. "[F]or the battle is the Lord's and He will give you [the adversary] into our hands." Note carefully that David said these words to Goliath as David took to the field with his proven sling.

[23] Second Timothy 1:7. See note 1, chapter 3.

[24] Second Timothy 1:7. Ibid.

[25] This partial quotation is taken from Hebrews 4:12 and is a verse that speaks of the ability of God's Word to discern and divide the deepest meditations and motivations of the human heart. The moral reach of the Bible sounds the depth of human thought and is able, promptly, to render a verdict as either right or wrong in the sight of both man and God.

[26] Colossians 2:9, 10. Speaking of Jesus Christ, Scripture teaches that the *pleroma*, or fullness of God, dwells in Him. The same word we apply to the Holy Bible as being inspired (*theopneustos*), fully (*pleroma*), or completely. Jesus is fully and completely God in the flesh and as such is sufficient for all that we (saints and non-saints, alike) need. Specifically, Christ's rule and authority is said to be over all, leaving no doubt from the text who Jesus Christ is and what that means to the vitality of His people.

[27] Psalm 19:8. This verse speaks to the source of true and lasting joy, together with the source of all genuine enlightenment. The statutes and commandments of the Lord suggest divine revelation as pure directives that sound the depths of the human vacuum for enduring joy and wisdom.

[28] First Timothy 5:23. What we have here is hardly a blanket permission for the use of strong drink or intoxicants. Paul is giving some literal and practical counsel to Timothy in view of his frequent infirmities. It is unlikely Paul is sanctioning wine usage for anything more than an inoculation against the effects of the lousy water Timothy was drinking (i.e., "no longer drink water only").

[29] Proverbs 31:4–7. It would appear, at first glance, that the Bible would encourage the use of intoxicants to drown out the oppressing cares of life. Our Proverb text is not to be understood, however, as an indiscriminate license for drinking, drunkenness, or the use of stimulants.

Proverbs 31 could be entitled "Advice for a King." The counsel of our text is thought to be that of Bathsheba, wife of David; the recipient is believed to be Solomon (or King Lemuel, by pseudonym). In any case, the king is warned against drinking either wine or strong drink since it is important for kings to have clear minds in the administration of their office (Prov. 31:4, 5). Intemperance lends itself to the inability to impartially evaluate hard questions. Intoxication will induce men to "pervert judgment" and thus neglect the cause of the afflicted and oppressed. A drunken king may easily reward the wicked and take away the righteousness of the righteous! The use of stimulants, like wine and strong drink, for reasons of pleasure and merriment are forbidden to kings. Intoxicating beverage is likewise forbidden to all others who would tarry long at the bottle for no other purpose than to party (Prov. 23:30). Since believers are made kings and priests unto God (Rev. 1:6), the command of abstinence is not far-fetched (Eph. 5:18).

Now, what about the permission of Proverbs 31:6, 7? To rightly divide this text, one must understand that strong drink and wine refer only to medicinal purposes. In early times, wine served humanity as a primary medicine to relieve serious pain and to calm the heart laden with bitter anguish (1 Tim 5:23). Proverbs recommends that the king should use the intoxicants as a cordial, or a medicine—either to ease the affliction of the dying (Matt. 27:34), or to lift the spirit of one who suffers bitter anguish of soul. The point is, such stimulants are to be used for medicinal purposes, never for mere partying!

What about the use of stimulants for the relief of depression, anxiety, or traumatic conditions of the mind and heart? We can accept the use of drugs to deaden the pain of a dying cancer patient, but what about those who suffer conflicts of the mind? Does Proverbs 31:6, 7 sanction the use of chemical treatment, the use of a stimulant? The use of stimulants, in such cases, is always an option. However, manufactured chemicals today are very potent and often carry with them undesirable side effects, as well as the risk of becoming potential crutches, providing no lasting solution to the problems of the soul. With the abundance of New Testament revelation comes increased responsibility for Christians to deal with their problems by godly exercise (1 Tim 3:16; 2 Pe 1:3). Christians have their options, but as kings, we have the opportunity to draw upon the resources of the Spirit, rather than the props of man-brewed stimulants. Obedience is always the better way to affect behavior!

30 Ephesians 5:18. The Greek term translated *dissipation* in the NKJV refers to the fruit of drunkenness as being riotous, profligate, incorrigible, and dissolute. The point of the apostle has to do with influences. Intoxicants, or any other mind-altering substances, in and of themselves, do not advance the Spirit's objective of sanctification. The influence of God's Spirit is the only legitimate mind-bender. This is what God commands and allows. The filling of the Holy Spirit produces the affects that follow in verses 19–20 (i.e., spiritual song, a praise-filled heart, and a deferring spirit). Medical influences or psychotropic targeting of viable physiological issues still carry with them biblical warning labels. Let the user beware, but in such cases it is assuring to know that God also judges according to the purposes of the heart.

31 Second Peter 1:3. The divine enablement, which is promised to permeate every aspect of our lives and our pursuit of godliness, is said to come to us through the "knowledge of Him." The knowledge inferred is the experiential knowledge of divine revelation, specifically disclosed to our hearts and minds by "the exceeding great and precious promises" (v. 4). Again, these promises become the medium for empowered living, for the divine nature of verse four.

32 First Timothy 4:16. Since Timothy was a believer and an elder, the salvation to which Paul refers must be the sanctification aspect of salvation, rather than the justification aspect. Timothy is thus encouraged in the steady application of biblical doctrine for deliverance in a sanctifying way, both for himself and for those to whom he ministers. The text is a sure recipe for overcomers.

33 "Je pense, donc je suis," states the French philosopher, Descartes. "I think, therefore, I am."

34 First Samuel 17:40. Observe David's careful selection of weaponry. He is very intentional and quite confident in his God and in his means, as he "drew near to the Philistine."

35 Second Timothy 4:7. Find the meaning in its context, with note 22, chapter 4. Remember, Paul is reflecting upon his many skirmishes, conflicts, and struggles in context of his victories and mastery along life's front line. He has been embattled long enough now to know that his defenses were strong and the outcome was a statement of courage.

36 Exodus 16:3. This verse is probably the ground indictment of a complaining people. As with many other verses, the children of Israel wished to have lived out their impoverished existence in Egypt, rather than trust a God whom they could not see and whom they would not believe. A bird in the hand is worth two in the bush for Israel; it would be better to be back in Egypt, eating the pods that the pigs ate, than trust the unseen hand of Yahweh for His promised supply. Pure pragmatics was the attitude of this wandering people. Results—and results *now*—was their bent, sadly! Israel found it difficult to rely upon God's greater purposes of faith, even though His salvation was rock solid and self-evident!

37 Romans 12:2. Transformed thinking and transformed living can only be attained through mind renewal. Obviously, the renewal of which I speak is that which comes by thinking God's thoughts after Him. We know from this verse that this renewal results in proving, or "with the expectation of approving," says W. E. Vine, "that which is the good and acceptable and perfect will of God" (*Vines Expository Dictionary of New Testament Words*, Vol. 3, p. 226, on James 1:21).

[38] Peter 1:6, 7. How often have you heard a Christian say of his trials, "I don't need this"? Peter lends differing insight; in fact, he teaches the opposite. This is precisely why trials come. We *need* them! Trials are grievous, *lupe*, implying pain, either to the body or mind. Actually, the rendering here is "having been put to grief." This is none other than intentional pain, which might put God in an obscure light, were it not for His disclosure: God purposes, through pain, to perfect the likeness of Himself in His people. We cannot always see what God is forging when the fire gets hot, but this we know, a tempering is going on in the lives of Christ's own that will authenticate them in the end. See 1 Thessalonians 1:6, 7. Let me suggest that you do a study on the word *examples* found in 1 Thessalonians 1:7. The verses exude treasures relative to our lesson.

[39] Proverbs 15:23. This proverb needs little comment. The maxim expresses inward joy and the affirmation of a moral conscience in the heart of one who answers wisely.

CHAPTER 6

Lateral Help for Languishing Hearts

There are few maneuvers as dazzling to wrestling fans as the lateral drop. If it's executed right, the move will bring an opponent from the standing posture to his back in a split second with an exclamation point! There are few things so demoralizing to a wrestler than to have the move employed against you right off the whistle start of the match. Lateral movement is great when you're in tight, up close, and personal. Follow the drift? I think you will.

Over the years, I have assisted the coaching staff in the neighboring high schools of the churches in which I've served. Wrestling with the guys got me into the community and provided many opportunities to impact the kids, and sometimes their families, for Christ.

Once, I assisted a local high school for eight years and thoroughly enjoyed the team, which came from the cellar of our league to championship status. A special perk for me during those times was having my son participate in the practice sessions. Though Nathaniel was ineligible to compete since he was enrolled in our private Christian school, he joined me regularly for the practice routine with the team. The open circuit tournaments gave my son some incentive for the brutal sessions he endured, but the "lateral" fellowship between us in those days is something for which I am grateful to God.

Somewhere in those fleeting days, I took several of the varsity starters to a weekly clinic in a distant town. The clinic featured a world-class wrestler. This athlete was second in the World Cup tournament, champion of the Pan American Games, and at that time held the country's second spot as a freestyler of 163 lbs.

When the clinic ended one night, our featured clinician asked for any challengers. Now, when my son volunteered me, I had to reconsider right then and there if I had been responsible for exaggerating his dad's wrestling stories in this young man's mind.

Well, every dad should be a hero in his son's own eyes, right? Insane! I was forty-three; the freestyler was in his twenties. Sure, I was in fair shape for an old guy, running a six minute mile and prepping for a master's tournament, but my opponent was two weeks away from Olympic tryouts. Besides, the gym was packed with coaches, wrestlers, and, worst of all, members from my team. As I walked to the mat's circle, I asked myself the question I had asked so many times before, *why did I have to choose this foolish sport?*

The next thing I knew, the whistle blew, and our dance started. The match would be expeditious; this I calculated from my competitor's resumé. Like a flash, he was there—into me, close-up and tight. He had pulled me in for a throw, possibly over his head. And there it was. That's right, the lateral drop. But on this occasion it was not to his advantage; it was to mine!

I countered with a move my coach, George Radman (one of Michigan State's finest), had shown me long ago (thank you, George!). Down he went, straight to his back, and there he lay, tight in my grasp (believe me, it was a grasp of self-preservation). And there we stayed until I heard the Olympian-bound whispering in my ear, "I guess I could stay here all day."

No, the point was made; no sense lingering, so we broke. The gym was quiet while the champion followed me into the locker room, inquiring about my background. In all fairness, I must say that the next bout I would have with this man would be a lesson on perspective; he had his way with me, but we became friends thereafter. Truly, Rob was the better wrestler. He was in the big leagues, and God simply gave me an Abishai moment before my son.

Catch the lesson here. It's straight out of my experience with the knowledge of God: Serious help for the sufferer, lasting help for the languishing lies in lateral movement. You must not fear to step into the circle with God. It is imperative that you get up close and personal, tight in if you will, allowing His Holy Spirit to "come alongside you"[1] in a real and vital way.

This is the nature of God. He takes delight in fervent and impassioned encounters with His people. There is blessing, which enables grace and hope for whatever a day brings forth when God is pursued with Jacob's tenacity: "And He [God] said, 'Let Me go, for the day breaks.' But he [Jacob] said, 'I will not let You go unless You bless me!'"[2]

Doesn't it throw you to realize it was God Himself who said that Jacob "struggled with God ... and prevailed"?[3] Wow! Think on that! Jacob came to grips with God, and as a result, he gained princely status with the Almighty (i.e., Israel).[4]

Boy, more than anything in life, I want to prevail upon the Lord as did Jacob. Oh, not for some vain motivation, but to be so swept into the grasp of Jesus Christ by pursuant faith that I am pulled into His mind, His life, His realm. There's help here—more help than anything you'll ever find watching from the bleachers. Let me supply you with a few samplings of just what I mean.

No Illusion—In the Encounter with God's Spirit

> Having been born again, not of corruptible seed but incorruptible, through the Word of God which lives and abides forever. (1 Pet. 1:23)[5]

A true encounter with the living God begins with the apprehension of the gospel of Jesus Christ. Anything short of this is an illusion, although the experience may be a religious one.

The gospel of Jesus Christ is found early in St. John's record, and it lies smack dab in the context of Jesus talking to a veteran rabbi about his soul. Here is the redemptive disclosure Jesus shares with Nicodemus from John chapter 3 concerning Himself:

- Jesus claims that He came out of heaven as the Son of Man (v. 13). Obviously, Christ speaks to His incarnation or His in-the-flesh appearance into the course of human history. The wonderful truth concerning Jesus' manifestation in human form is delineated so abundantly from Philippians 2: 5–8.[6] A theological term that expresses well the union of both divine and human qualities in the person of Jesus Christ is called the hypostatic union, and our Philippian text uncovers this beautifully. The gospel writer has already unearthed the glory of Jesus, when in John 1:14[7] he demonstrates the uniqueness of the divine Logos becoming flesh.

- Jesus further claims that there was something remedial, something redemptive, yea, something salvific to His being lifted up, not unlike the serpent on the wilderness pole (Num 21:4–9).[8] The sight of the serpent brought healing to all those, who in faith, beheld the remedy (v. 14).

- Jesus claims that beholding Him in faith and in connection with the pole (or cross) would bring about eternal life, as opposed to being lost, or perishing (*apollumi*). Clearly, Jesus advocates that the salvific boon resides in His very person (v. 15).

- Jesus claims that God's motive for Christ's manifestation to the world is love. Jesus is actually the gift for everlasting life from the Almighty and believing the gift would divert any soul from destruction in due course (v. 16).

- Jesus claims that His mission in the first advent is saving, not condemning, but He reiterates the need for all humanity to believe into His name if they are to escape the obvious consequence of their own depravity (vv. 17, 18).

- Jesus claims, in finale, that all men are destitute of light and of truth and that innate, soulish darkness, or evil is the basis of universal condemnation before God (vv. 19–21).

These truths must have been tough stuff for the very religious rabbi, especially as the reader discovers that Jesus is exploiting Nicodemus' own desperate need. I mean, this discussion has no denominational dibs to it! The teaching belongs to the Lord of Glory, and conformity to its naked disclosure will immediately characterize truth from error, fact from fiction, light from darkness and reality from illusion.

Herein is objective truth: it is revelation from on high, and whether or not it is believed doesn't change the truth that Jesus disclosed these things about Himself. What Nicodemus found with Jesus Christ was no illusion; it was an objective encounter with a living reality.

To avoid encounter with God's Son is nothing less than unbelief in His veritable persona. All true conversion is thus a personal and redemptive encounter with Jesus Christ whose claims come out of an historical context and whose person must be trusted absolutely, or remain buried in unbelief. It is a denial such as this that is spiritually and morally ruinous to one's hope for atonement and eternal life, according to Jesus Christ.

The most important link to knowing God in a real and vital way, the cardinal axiom of all spiritual verity, is found early on in Jesus' discussion with Nicodemus. Before anything else is said, Jesus tells the religious leader that all legitimate experience with God, all authentic encounters with the God of heaven and earth, must come about and can only come about by God's Spirit.

Illustrating the effect of the Holy Spirit upon a life, Jesus taught from John 3:3–8:[9]

- The Holy Spirit awakes all genuine belief in Jesus Christ.
- The Holy Spirit authors all genuine spiritual life with God.
- The Holy Spirit produces all genuine experience of God.
- The Holy Spirit incites all genuine likeness to God.

The context reveals a forthright discussion on spiritual entities with a Jewish ruler. Jesus is setting forth His claims that are intrinsic to the biblical gospel.

The lament, however, which qualifies all sincere encounters with the true and living God, is resultant from and dependent upon the Holy Spirit who is sent from God. The Spirit of God blows life into an otherwise spiritual corpse (Eph 2:1),[10] but in connection with the gospel of Jesus Christ (Rom 10:8–17),[11] i.e., the saving claims of His person.

The apprehension of Jesus Christ through the Holy Spirit is no illusion. It's the real thing, and it begins with the gospel. There, God Himself is encountered in a justifying way and in a life-changing way. The initial encounter gives assurance that God is real, life has purpose, and eternity is in our soul. The world may deny it; the skeptic may dismiss it as purely subjective or a figment of an imaginative mind. The truth is that the encounter is consistent with objective revelation.

The encounter with God is true to the experience of millions and when you embrace the reality of Jesus Christ by the gospel: you know that you know. The words of Evan H. Hopkins seem fitting:

> You may put a telescope into the hands of a man who is blind, and bid him look at some distant star, or on some lovely landscape. He tells you he sees nothing. Well, his witness is true. So the agnostic affirms of all supernatural religion that he knows it not.

> His witness also is true. But, if the blind man goes further and asserts that because he sees nothing, there is nothing to see; his assertion is untrue and his witness is worthless because he speaks beyond the range of his capacity.
>
> Such is the value of the natural man's opinion when he declares his mind on spiritual things. But the natural may become spiritual. The spiritually blind man may be restored to sight. The agnostic who knows not may be brought to see and understand and know.[12]

I remember the testimonial that one of our church members shared with me some time ago regarding his justifying encounter with God (coming to grips with God for the first time). Believing Christ's claims from the heart, having been awakened by God's own Spirit, this man put his faith and confidence in the living Jesus. With joy and excitement, the man shared his experience with his priest.

"I've been born again," said this man with the quickened heart.

"That's a Protestant expression," said the priest, and that was all there was to it—a Protestant expression.

Honestly, I've heard that sort of thing before from various denominational stripes. The problem here is that spiritual rebirth is a Jesus doctrine! It is a clear teaching straight from the mouth of Jesus Christ. It is the declaration of the church on the move in the book of Acts. It is the exposition of epistolary literature. The wonderful, but dreadful, statement of fact from the lips of Christ Jesus is undisguised, "Most assuredly I say to you, unless one is born again, he cannot see the kingdom of God."[13]

Neither pope nor pastor, neither priest nor parishioner, nor may anyone belonging to Adam's posterity hope for heaven without "repentance toward God and faith toward our Lord Jesus Christ" (Acts 20:21).[14] But, of course, this whole-hearted embrace with the Redeemer is a Holy Spirit thing, hence, spiritual rebirth, or (lit.)

"birth from above,"[15] or regeneration[16]—all of these renderings speak of the same encounter or experience of knowing Christ in an immediate and salvific way.

I did not intend this book to be a treatise on soteriology. The beautiful language of Scripture has been sweet to me as I've enjoyed those expositional labors incumbent upon a pastor and servant of God. Hard work in the text has only heightened the joy of what the Holy Spirit did in my life as a young man. What has been given by grace can never be taken away by a mocking world as I realize, time and time again, that people are naturally skeptical of what they do not understand.

No illusion here! And what does this mean for the combatant, the believer struggling with life, with fears? It means that nothing in my life happens purely by accident. It means the universe about me is not simply random, molecular, or a cud-chewing monster. It means that my whole existence makes too much sense to mean nothing! It means there is a moral Sovereign who lives enthroned at the center of it all and He is my inheritance by birthright!

Bring it on! Let this encounter with God sweep me into His fullness where, "I shall know just as I also am known" (1 Cor. 13:12).[17] Come into the circle, friend, and take a knee. "Beloved, now we are children of God; and it has not yet been revealed what we shall be, but we know that when He is revealed, we shall be like Him, for we shall see Him as He is" (1 John 3:2).[18]

No Sorrow—in the Pursuit of God's Favor

> Their sorrows shall be multiplied who hasten after another god; their drink offerings of blood I will not offer, nor take up their names on my lips. (Ps 16:4)[19]

Someone has said that the primary yearning of humanity has always been peace of mind. Philosophers, poets, and logicians have said it; likewise, all those who observe and mark the human experience concur that the pinnacle aspiration of mankind is peace of mind.

The pursuit of happiness may dominate the practical focus of most people; yet peace of mind must be the ultimate motivation of man's fixation with his own happiness. To reach a state of utter contentment would characterize heaven to most people. Heaven, to them, would thus be a place where the mind resides in perpetual contentment, the place where happiness settles upon sublime serenity.

History gives clear testimony to man's search for tranquility of soul. He has sought it through education, material wealth (like winning the power ball lottery), military might, hallucinogens, music, human relationships, athleticism, youth feats and accomplishments—along with a myriad of other dead-end roads that promise peace and happiness. The commentary of human history tells us over and over again that peace of mind escapes mankind.

There seems to be no real solution to man's practical dilemma; no ultimate satisfaction! The songs of our culture tell us this. Social discontentment shouts it. The entertainment craze seeks to mask it and laugh at it but only desensitizes us to it. The prophet Isaiah, however, makes an accurate observation about it! The predicament of the natural man is "like the troubled sea, when it cannot rest, whose waters cast up mire and dirt" (Isa 57:20).[20]

Frankly, humanity has always been in mass denial, because man is innately born in despair and without hope. When he banks on hope within himself, or with someone or something else, he is at best despairing confidently, for he knows life turns up empty. There is a vacuum within that he must attempt to fill with idolatries, and yet peace of mind continues to evade his grasp.

Now, I have met people who have told me that they are basically happy with life. We all would admit to a relative happiness, for as long as things go well, life is great, so we say. But receive a cancer diagnosis from the family physician or, as was the case with my son and his dear wife, receive the heartbreaking news that your sons would pass away early in their childhood years, then—well, life is neither happy nor peaceful. There is, of course, happiness by pretense only; it seems everybody's fine and good until you get beneath the surface and converse honestly. Happiness is an elusive thing because, observably, it appears to be circumstantial to most.

There is no sorrow with Jesus Christ. In the sense that He is an offense to the world, there is a reproach His people pick up that becomes, at times, grievous. But, in the person of Christ, the search for completeness ends. Bathing in the fullness of the divine qualities satisfies. There is simply no defection when one is close with the heart of God, because the soul has returned home to the "peace I give to you." Jesus said that the peace He gives is "not as the world gives do I give you. Let not your heart be troubled, neither let it be afraid" (John 14:27).[21]

Folks have asked me over the years whether I have delved into the insights of other religions, of other gods. Certainly as a college and seminary student I've done the academic assignments and have also been exposed to the world of religious thought as a pastor. I have been alert to the end-time prophets, have heard their claims, have read their treatises, and have brought their lives against the words of Jesus and the plumb line of His life. Truthfully, defection has never been an option.

You see, once you've found the real thing, why jump ship? What else could I find that could possibly give me more than what I enjoy in union with the Author of my existence? Can I learn more from an open, eclectic approach toward the world about me? My response: why truncate my heart and mind by inculcating that which is not from Him "in whom are hidden all the treasures of wisdom and knowledge" (Col 2:3)?[22]

To me, it is a narrowing of my knowledge, of my understanding, of my intellect to succumb to philosophical minutiae. Apart from that which is "not according to Christ" (Col 2:8),[23] my mind lays hold on themes that are out of this world, and the most scholarly have on occasion taken notice of those lives who have so learned Christ (Acts 4:13).[24] Indeed, all truth is Jehovah's truth, and all knowledge is but God thinking. There is a vast reservoir of knowledge in God; the depths of His knowledge and wisdom can never be sounded (Rom 11:33).[25]

My high school years were not my best years academically. I graduated near the tail end of the grade point standings in my class. The school counselor and academic advisor asked me to talk with him in his office, which I was happy to do—after all, I was college bound. To my surprise, the counselor told me, without any attempt to cloak his words, that, "Mark, I don't believe you are college material."

Now, I was a nice kid, a varsity wrestler, but that doesn't float well when you haven't invested yourself in the study end of things. Deep down inside, those comments didn't send me into despair, because I knew for certain that God was directing my life toward ministry, and I knew the issue of academics was something of negligence on my part. This was an area I had to resolve with my God.

Education was necessary to my calling, and God was at the center of this discipline. So I yielded this achievement up to Him, went to college on academic probation, and spent my first few undergraduate years learning how to study. Graduating as a merit student, I took a pastorate and studied God's Word, generally, most of the daylight hours. The evenings I would spend with family, in outreach, and in other pastoral duties.

During this season of life, the Lord enabled me to complete a seminary program and finish course work in biblical counseling. I even faced off again with Greek, but this time Attic Greek at Cornell University—partly for the challenge of gaining strength in a study that always took me to the mat.

Now, it was at about this time that the superintendent of my public high school asked me to come back and address the juniors and seniors. Can you believe it? At my own high school only a dozen years later, and now speaking from the head of the class!

Addressing the students, I noticed my former academic counselor standing at the very back of the large library room. When I was finished with my challenge, off I went to catch my advisor, but he was nowhere to be found. I wanted to tell him that though his counsel was based on observable data, there remains the element of the unseen and the element of surprise with God! His fullness transforms lives!

Occasionally (as I prepare for a radio talk show, or write some article for a periodical, or prepare for a speaking engagement), I muse at what coming into favor with Jesus Christ can do. It's *all* of grace, as Charles H. Spurgeon entitled one of his most helpful works so many years before.[26]

Amazing, isn't it? I wouldn't trade anything else for the joy of knowing Him, of being close in! I wouldn't exchange the tinsel pleasures of this passing world for my adventurous, thrilling, and fulfilling attachment to Jesus Christ. This life with Him is abundantly above what I could ever ask or think (Eph 3:20).[27]

Settling upon our immediate thought, I want to share the peace of God that my son, Nathaniel, passed on to his readers when his beloved son and our grandson, Titus, struggled to survive his first fourteen weeks among us.

> There have been many things to praise the Lord for. However, the past few weeks have not gone so well. The first two brain surgeries did not work out, so a couple of days ago Titus was given a VP shunt. It's a spaghetti-shaped tube, complete with pump valve, that connects to one of his ventricles (which produces brain fluid) and runs down behind his ear through his chest, draining into the stomach area.
>
> It's barely visible, but it is permanent. Word on the street is they're very fragile and break easily.

We were hoping this would have an immediate positive result, but since the surgery, Titus has been having severe apnea. They have had to "bag him" (pump oxygen into his lungs) several times. I was there for a couple of these episodes (and Kim, more) and it was extremely scary.

In light of this, Titus had to have an EEG test where they taped a bunch of colorful wires to his head to read his brain waves (making sure they're not seizures). There is not a disingenuous fiber in my being when I say that God has recently impressed me with this reality: If Kim and I truly believe that God ordains trials for the purpose of making us like Christ and understanding Him better (which is the most noble endeavor, period), then every detail of this fourteen-week whirlwind is one massive expression of God's love. How else do we "count it all joy?"

The truly unfortunate among us are those who go through life never realizing this."

God allowed our disabled, sweet "Triumphant Titus" to gift us with four and a half years of joy and of learning to lean hard on the God of all comfort, the God of all sufficient grace. Today, Titus is home with Jesus. No hopeless sorrow! His home going was followed by one of the most passionate messages I have ever given, and not solely because our beloved Titus was my grandson, but largely because my God is "not the God of the dead, but the God of the living" (Mt 22:32).[28]

Titus walks among the wise today and I know this to be true. You see, there is a provision in Christ's atonement for the child who "cannot discern between their right hand and their left" (Jonah 4:11).[29]

Some time ago, I was able to settle upon the doctrine of destiny for young children, infants, and the unborn. I have a theological premise for hope, joy, and peace of mind that is based on inspired line, not unstable feelings. This young heritage with the golden laugh serves the God I know and serve today. What kind of being can give that assurance? Is there any rival to Him?

Up to this point, all creation has played in the minor key (Rom 8:22),[30] but the promise of the living God has fallen upon the children of God (Rom 8:2),[31] granting them a lively hope that replaces sorrow with the joy of His presence (John 15:10, 11;[32] Rom 14:17;[33] 1 Th 1:6;[34] He 12:2;[35] 1 Pet. 1:8).[36]

In the pursuit of God there is no enduring sorrow, and to cut to the quick, there is no reasonable basis for irrational fears! Bottom line, the oppressive picture I paint upon the walls of my mind is imagined. The picture is a heart construct and about as substantial as a shadow.

Close in the circle of God's favor, nothing befalls His sons that is not orchestrated to make us accomplished in the pursuit of God Himself (Phlp 3:12).[37] Engrafting this truth to my heart and mind is sufficient to counter the dreaded prospect of another ominous, fear-filled day. There is peace in the valley for me, and God Himself ensures the outcome! "[B]elieve in the Lord your God, and you shall be established ..." (2 Chr 20:20).[38]

No Fear—In the Grip of Love

> Who shall separate us from the love of Christ?
> (Rom 8:35a)[39]

One further blessing, and quite possibly the most comforting, comes from the assurance that we are objects of Christ's love. This lateral movement of the Holy Spirit is experienced daily by those close up with God and held tight by His own grip. There is much about God's love for His own from the pages of Holy Scripture.

Several portions from the epistles lend deeper insight into this attachment of love that believers enjoy with their heavenly Father. For example, contemplate the following:

First: There is no basis to fear the wrath or judgment of God any longer. "There is no fear in love ..." (1 John 4:18a).[40] The Greek term for fear in the verse is *phobos*, and it carries with it the idea of terror, or dread. In ancient times, its use suggested the act of taking flight and not as the Wright brothers, but flight as in running scared. You'll note the previous verse speaks of the day of judgment,[41] so we know that the specific inference to fear would convey to us that the love of God negates the terror of coming judgment upon the believing soul. May I add that the believer's struggle with irrational fear is not symptomatic of condemnation? The grip of God's love secures every hope of future dwelling with Jesus Christ.

Second: There is every reason to believe that love is a viable antidote to fear. "Perfect love casts out fear" (1 John 4:18b).[42] In this immediate case, love that has matured, or the life that is abiding with God is enabled to dispel the dread of God, or the haunting terror of coming judgment upon one's own soul. Herein is an applicatory principle for all fears. The abiding love of God within is greater than inner human fears, which Scripture tells us do not come from God (2 Tim 1:7).[43]

Love is a communicable attribute of the Almighty,[44] and so it is strong to overpower the fearful heart of abiding saints. Here's how it works: I have gone to the pulpit scared and fearful. Grasping the lectern, I have peered at my audience many times with this thought: *What this audience needs to hear is this message of grace. Christ's own sheep are seated before me. God loves them and has sent me to feed them.*

What I do at this point in my self-talk is something I've designed for myself, but I do get very directive with myself and say something like this: *Mark, quit being so self-absorbed. Focus on the sheep and not on how you're feeling; besides, if you choke, well, you'll just have to choke, so start feeding the flock.*

How many times I have been delivered by love! That is, simply loving others and obediently acting upon the love of God.[45] Love is a wonderful antidote for fear, and this truth can be applied in so many ways to defeat a conquerable adversary.

Third: There is nothing of substance to the notion that the fear episode is impenetrable to God's love!

We sort of think, at times, that once a fear event is in motion, the mechanics of the episode take over. Once more, the Bible teaches otherwise. In Romans, chapter 8, the apostle Paul, under the direction of the Holy Spirit, goes to great pains delineating what extremes might tempt the Christian to doubt God's love toward them. "Who [or what] shall separate us from the love of Christ?" Paul asks (v. 35). And here come the apparent threats:

- *Tribulation* (v. 35): *Thlipsis* is a general Greek term for affliction of all sorts. It is used by Paul for the many things he suffered along the gospel road throughout his years of service (Eph 3:13).[46] It is also used in 2 Corinthians 1:4,[47] where the apostle relates the term *thlipsis* to "any trouble" befalling God's people. So then, any form of affliction, trouble, suffering, torment, or the like—yea, none of these are severe enough to limit love's access to our situation. Truly, our tribulations are not impervious to God's love!

- *Distress* (v. 35): *Stenochoria* is a very special word to me. The noun comes from two Greek words, *stenos* (narrow) and *chora* (place). This must be a claustrophobic term. It is a tight place, a narrow area that results in anguish. You can see how the noun's metaphorical use relates a feeling to the meaning of distress. Once again, God's love is sure, certain and effectual, even in the tight places of life. In fact, anguish may come, as the verse implies, but it doesn't change the believer's relationship with God, nor does the narrow place seal out love's enabling reach.

- *Persecution* (v. 35): The Greek meaning here suggests being driven out. The reason for persecution is evident: the gospel. There is a sharp edge to the gospel that makes enemies, as well as converts. The historical context of the early church out of the book of Acts reinforces this, time after time. In those very times when it seems we are all alone or at best few in number, when it appears we are quite unpopular with the consensus and the social drift would have us hide our gospel under a bushel; in such times of being ostracized—the love of Jesus Christ is strong, constant, and unaffected.

- *Famine* (v. 35): Dearth, hunger, famine—these various translations for the Greek word *limos* all speak of those harsh conditions where the soul might be tempted to question the love of God. Seeing that famine follows hard upon persecution, *limos* may lend the idea of hunger, or scarcity of food, brought about by our gospel witness. In any case, the absence of bread is never symptomatic of the absence of love. When we are in the golden chain of God's redemption (vv. 29, 30),[48] divine love is irrevocable.

- *Nakedness* (v. 35): Most likely, the emphasis here would lie in the inability of one to cover one's own body with adequate clothing. When it comes down to this, things are pretty dire, wouldn't you agree? Things may look dire, but God-ward things look very good. Love will secure for the child of grace all that is necessary for the greater good of God's merciful purposes toward His own. This truth is a certainty.

- *Peril* (v. 35): The synonym for peril is danger. Danger, of whatever kind, is a stimulus for fear. Peril, however, would infer a real and imminent danger that might result in personal harm and injury. Unlike irrational fears, which may be generated from stimuli that hold no real danger, our text speaks of true peril. Yet here in the heat of a viable affront to our well-being, God's love is said to be joined fast to our lives. It is not peeled away by whatever danger might tilt our sanity.

- *Sword* (v. 35): In contrast to the Thracian weapon of warfare, this noun is rendered from a word that generally refers to a dagger or even a knife. It implies a murderous use. The sword is a killing instrument. Paul uses this word to impress upon the minds of his readers a sense of finality at the merciless hands of men. But even this does not separate us from "the love of God which is in Christ Jesus" (v. 39).

Once the apostle dismisses the potential threats upon the believer's assurance of being divinely loved, he further fleshes out more particulars, or extremes if you will, which are likewise impotent to disturb God's love for us, "[N]either death nor life ... nor any other created thing ..." (vv. 38, 39).[49]

What more could possibly be said that the apostle Paul has not touched upon? His point is obvious: there is nothing, nothing that can subdue us in life, not to the greatest expanse of heaven above, nor to the depths of the earth beneath. Whether in our life's existence or in the mystery of death, whether visible or invisible or anything created by God Himself (even including the evil that is subject to His decree), nothing is able to sever us from His love!

Believers, as sons of God, are hemmed in by God's love through the gospel. In fact, life trauma doesn't change the status of God's elect. We may lose sight of God's love in our madness, but God never loses sight of us in His providential watch care.

What a wonderful teaching upon which to meditate day and night! It is this strong mooring of the mind that brings so much gravity to a disconcerted heart. Just imagine the comfort Psalm 23 brought to the heart of King David. In all that befell this hunted, hated, esteemed, and revered man, David was sustained by the love of God, which comes to expression so vividly in the twenty-third Psalm.[50]

Throughout the inspired lines, the psalmist writes, sings, or commands his composers to fill up His courts with praise. The unvaried theme of the lyric is God's merciful attention to the details of his own life. David wrestles so often to stay afloat amid heavy distress, persecution, famine, nakedness, peril, and sword. How refreshing that the final five chapters belonging to the book of the Psalms begin with *Hallelujah*[51] (Hebrew) and end with the same!

Into this circle of lateral fellowship with God there is answer and purpose for my existence. There is joy and peace in my days; no more emptiness as with the song of fools. Finally, there is a covenant of love upon my soul and such that cannot be changed in time and in eternity. These blessed elements of grace grant me the mental fortitude needed to embrace life as an overcomer. These blessed provisions must also be nurtured daily if I am to be made ready for the race ahead. Let me speak briefly to this subject of day-to-day endurance.

There are four activities in our closing discussion that are needful for nurturing empowered living. We have said already that stepping into that intimate circle with God begins with the gospel of Jesus Christ. Faith, however, like repentance, is not only the initial feature of grace, but faith is also the sustaining element of grace.

Scripture plainly teaches us that the faith belonging to God's elect (as opposed to the faith of demons, James 2:19,[52] or the faith of Simon of Samaria, Acts 8:13)[53] is pursuant to godliness (Titus 1:1).[54] Godliness, or the pursuit of God likeness, is the authenticating telltale characteristic of genuine conversion (Eph. 2:10).[55] The fruits always speak of the roots. A tree is known by the fruit it bears. Jesus said, "Therefore, by their fruits you will know them" (Matt. 7:20).[56]

Since true saints are made alive to God's glory, fruit bearing, or God likeness, is both an admonition and a certainty (Phlp 2:12, 13).[57] Such being the case, I know of only four resources that God has chosen to sustain the troops, making them sanctified and useful for the Master (2 Tim 2:21).[58] These resources are well known to the troops and probably need more use among the ranks than our endearing expressions about them. They are:

1. *The Bible*, God's Holy Word (2 Tim 3:16, 17):[59] All that I need to make me complete (mature) and equipped for every service to Christ comes to me in connection with the regular and faithful ingestion of this Book.

2. *Prayer* (1 Th 5:17):[60] Praying the mind of Holy Scripture to a personal God is life-penetrating and life-changing. Prayer takes us into a realm above and beyond our temporal and self-absorbed world to a plane of knowledge that keeps us waiting on God. It's simply a livelier level of being.

3. *The church*, Christ's body (He 10:24, 25):[61] The right church makes all the difference in the world. Don't look for a church free of conflict. Conflict is needful for maturity. Look for a church body that demonstrates the dynamics of Acts 2:41–49,[62] where doctrine is the first thing. Discern between ministries that simply talk about the Bible from ministries that let the truth stand in its proper biblical context. Submit yourself to scrutiny under church elders so that the mutual support and accountability of shepherds can assist your sanctification and service.

4. *The Holy Spirit* (Rom 8:14):[63] The Holy Spirit's work is inseparable from the aforementioned. He must be obeyed

if we are to be led along. There is no greater resource to the Christian than the lateral help coming from God's own Spirit. Here is sufficient enablement for all who are held close in to God's heart. In a real sense, then, harnessing fear becomes an issue of personal maturity, especially as we consult the nature of our divine inhabitant.

My thoughts travel back years ago to a lady whom I deeply respected for her passion for Jesus. I had engaged her in the counseling room, and my wife enjoyed an ongoing mentorship with her.

She had come to an impasse with her husband. There were definitive communication impediments between them, and she could not hurdle them by all the means and methods I could supply. Long she had sought a key to the breakthrough, a silver bullet through the ongoing sessions that might break her free, set her loose.

One day, I put it kindly, but straight, as I told her, "There's nothing more I can do for you." I remember that she appeared shocked and slightly hurt.

Eventually, my wife and I left the area for another ministry. Our lives with this dear saint did not intersect again until somewhere, someplace, she approached me. After our initial greeting and not too far into our conversation, she made a statement I cannot forget: "When you told me there was no more that you could do for me, it hit me as it never had before," she expressed. "You could not help me beyond what I must resolve to do myself before God."

She went on to explain that her relationship with her husband had grown and that her life with God was growing as well. And just maybe (satirically speaking) the reverse order was true—her life with God was growing and, consequently, her relationship with her husband.

When you venture to move in on God without all the excuses and demands of human insecurities, the encounter gets very personal; faith is enlarged and help is meted out from God's own hand. In prostrate dependence upon His resources, God will act to give His pursuer a Peniel moment (Gen 32:30),[64] where he or she will be blessed to know the One with whom he or she has been wrestling.

Chapter Six Endnotes

[1] John 14:26. Parakletos (Gk.), called to one's side. Literally, the word identifies the Holy Spirit with an appellation of ministry, namely, helper (NKJV).

[2] Genesis 32:26. Jacob's Peniel experience where he encountered God in His struggle for divine favor.

[3] Genesis 32:28. See the following footnote.

[4] Genesis 32:28. The renaming of Jacob by God Himself was the evident blessing Jehovah left behind with His disappearance at dawn. The name, Israel, means "prince with God," as Jacob received with it posterity and a future inheritance in Zion. The tenacity of Jacob's faith prevailed upon God. See Hebrews 11:6.

[5] First Peter 1:23. Born-again, or begotten again, (lit.) from the Greek word *gennao*. Here, our verse says that it is the incorruptible Word of God, which is living and abiding, that brings about spiritual life to the soul. In contrast to the decay of a natural seed, God's Word engenders eternal life through, or by means of faith (cp Rom. 10:17).

[6] Philippians 2:5–8. Two great doctrines surrounding the incarnate, or in-the-flesh appearance of God into the course of human history are found here: first, the hypostatic union, or the wonder of Jesus Christ's existence as fully man, yet fully God in the same Person; second, the kenosis of our Lord, or His stripping. The idea renders a composite of Jesus as veiled Deity. As God, Jesus is stripped, or humbled, by assuming the servant role of man. The stripping was consensual, but voluntary in connection with the Trinity.

7   John 1:14. The *Logos* (Gk.) of the passage that the gospel writer identifies as Jesus Christ (v. 17) is uniquely God the Son and Son of God: this "Word" of John, chapter 1, literally tabernacled in the flesh among men. He also gave expression to God's glorious image by fully emitting in His earthly person all grace and truth.

8   Numbers 21:4–9. The event of the healing serpent in the wilderness wanderings became a type of His own saving remedy through the cross, according to Jesus. There are many correlations to the episode of the fiery serpent and the smitten Savior. In either case, faith in the provision that Jehovah supplied was the basis for deliverance. It has always amazed me that Jesus became such a gross spectacle by His crucifixion. Has it ever occurred to you that in becoming sin for us, God's only Son fulfilled the typology of Moses' smitten serpent on a pole (Isa 53:4, 5)? Truly, a spectacle of grace!

9   John 3:3–8. Herein is Jesus' first lesson for Nicodemus concerning his personal salvation. The Savior begins with an explanation concerning the place of the Holy Spirit in true conversion. According to the text, the Spirit's place is paramount, pervasive, and particular to legitimate union with Christ.

10   Ephesians 2:1. See again note 1, chapter 4.

11   Romans 10:8–17. All ten verses penned by the apostle Paul spell out clearly the fundamental elements that are involved in the soul's justification before God. These elements include: (1) the Word of faith that we preach (v. 8); (2) the confession of the mouth to the Lord Jesus Christ and the heart belief in His resurrection reality (v. 9); (3) belief unto righteousness and confession unto salvation (v. 10); (4) salvific deliverance resultant from a personal call or cry to the Lord (vv. 12, 13); (5) the hearing of a heralded message that leads to the saving cry of faith (vv. 14, 15); and (6) obedient faith spawned by the hearing of God's Word (vv. 16, 17). In connection with our Lord's teaching from John 3, all theological elements that are necessary to conversion expect, suppose, or assume Holy Spirit awakening. This awakening involves the apprehension of the biblical Christ in both heart and mind.

[12] Evan A. Hopkins, *The Law of Liberty in the Spiritual Life* (Toronto, Canada: University of Toronto Libraries, 2011) internet accessed, June 23, 2013.

The author has found several helpful insights from the writings of Evan H. Hopkins. As a leading proponent of the theological perspective known as "Keswick thinking," however, I would advise a critical sift through his works.

[13] John 3:3. An imperative statement by the Lord Jesus Christ.

[14] Acts 20:21. In an address to the Ephesian elders at Miletus, the apostle Paul summarizes the testament of Christ that he preaches to both the Jews and Greeks (i.e., "repentance toward God and faith toward our Lord Jesus Christ").

[15] John 3:3. *Born again* may be translated "born from above" (Gk., *anothen*).

[16] Titus 3:5. Actually, the word rendered regeneration could be properly translated *reborn*, or (lit), *again begotten*.

[17] First Corinthians 13:12. Heaven knows the elect offspring of Jehovah to be the sons of God. The full revelation of sonship is yet virtually unknown by the redeemed. Whatever knowledge of what we are and of what we've become by grace is afforded by the Holy Spirit in concert with objective truth. It is thus logical to assume that the measure of any saint's intimacy with Jesus Christ lies in the depth of one's intimate knowledge of God and the knowledge of oneself in relationship to God. Moving closer to God's heart is revealing on both counts—His and ours!

[18] First John 3:2. The full revelation of sons awaits the believer's final glorification. The ultimate conformity to Christ that every Christian will experience does not disallow progressive conformity and maturity in the knowledge of God now. Sons of God may look increasingly like God in their moral stature now. Sons of God may grow in the knowledge of the Holy more fully with every passing day (2 Pe. 3:18).

[19] Psalm 16:4. A god is anything that preempts the throne in one's life where the biblical God should alone reign supreme. Plainly, all other pursuits apart from the true and living God are here portrayed as roads of multiplied sorrows.

[20] Isaiah 57:20. Here is a description of the transgressor who is as troubled waters. Restlessness and inner turmoil characterize the life that resists God.

[21] John 14:27. The peace Christ affords through the agency of His Spirit is fuller, richer, and deeper than what the world can ever give. The verse concludes with the imperative from Jesus, who commands His own not to be troubled or fearful.

[22] Colossians 2:3. The Scripture at hand speaks directly of Jesus Christ as the source of all true wisdom and knowledge. One may conclude, then, that unless Jesus is at the center of all learning and understanding, such education, then, is deficient.

[23] Colossians 2:8. The search for wisdom and knowledge that rules out the centrality of Jesus Christ is, in the final analysis, philosophy that cheats its students from real learning. All such philosophy is said to be merely from the tenants of the world, humanistic and hollow. The Greek text is very colorful in its denouncement of philosophy which is not after Christ.

[24] Acts 4:13. Peter and John, being in the fishing trade, were perceived by their contemporaries as uneducated and untrained men. Their knowledge of Jesus and communion with Him brought amazement to the minds of men in regard to both the substance and power of their oratory. The text tells us how the educated and elite among Israel realized that they had been with Jesus. This result can be anticipated when you are close to God.

[25] Romans 11:33. The unfathomable depths of God's wisdom and knowledge are extolled by Paul. The judgments of God are also said to be beyond the range of man's ability to search them out. Essentially, the verse lauds God's omniscience.

[26] Spurgeon, Charles. *All of Grace*. Chicago, Ill.: Moody Publishers, 2010. Internet accessed, June 26, 2013.

[27] Ephesians 3:20. The verse is a promise waiting to be realized in its application by those in union with Christ.

[28] Matthew 22:32. As Jesus addresses the subject of the resurrection, He discloses that the dead always live before an ever-present God. Not only is

future resurrection implied, but God relates now to His covenant people in a vital fellowship sense, even though they are "dead" (i.e., Abraham, Isaac, and Jacob).

29. Jonah 4:11. A parallel reference to this verse is Deuteronomy 1:39, where similar language identifies children, or little ones as those who cannot discern right or wrong. Seeing that population estimates of Nineveh number more than a half million people, we may safely assume the verse speaks of children. God is evidently reproving Jonah's lack of mercy toward little ones, numbering 120,000 strong, as Jonah grudgingly contemplates God sparing the evil city from judgment.

30. Romans 8:22. Actually, all creation is in labor with the accompanying groans of pain and discomfort, awaiting the delivery or the resurrection of redeemed sons. Once delivered, the corruption and bondage associated with the world of sin will be cut loose and creation, together with the redeemed sons of God, will be forever set at liberty.

31. Romans 8:2. Through the gospel of our salvation, the law that has been written in our hearts by the Holy Spirit has loosed the converts of Jesus from the death sentence of God's law upon their lives. See also Romans 8:1.

32. John 15:10, 11. Keeping the commandments of Jesus Christ assures the abiding love of God, as well as the experience of the Savior's very own joy.

33. Romans 14:17. The qualities of righteousness, peace, and joy characterize the kingdom of God and come to heaven's citizens by the Holy Spirit.

34. First Thessalonians 1:6. More witness to the joy of God's presence within the heart of God's people! Here, the joy of the Holy Spirit is seen in afflicted saints with whom Paul rejoices.

35. Hebrews 12:2. Christ's own joy as He faced the cross is commended of us. The joy of Christ is the substance of the heart of all grace runners and finishers.

36. First Peter 1:8. Joy inexpressible and full of glory is the atmosphere of faith abiding in all who believe in Christ's future revelation.

37 Philippians 3:12. Paul is pressing toward perfection in keeping with the constraint of grace. Seeing that the constraint is of God and consistent with God's purpose of predestination (i.e., Christ likeness), the apostle persevered in the course of adversity by desire and design. See also note 21, chapter 4.

38 Second Chronicles 20:20. Jehoshaphat's pronouncement to Judah just prior to God's destruction of the people of Ammon, Moab, and Mount Seir. While Judah and the inhabitants of Jerusalem offered up praises of faith to God, the Lord Himself ambushed Judah's enemies and wasted them in the wilderness of Tekoa.

39 Romans 8:35a. The interrogative is intended as a summons or a challenge for saints to bring anything to the table that might seem to threaten the strength of God's love toward His elect children. The apostle is about to measure up all that is against the saints in this realm of conflict. He will proceed, then, to debunk any suggestion that anyone of God's own stands in jeopardy of a disconnect from God's love. The simple answer to Paul's summons is a repetitive neither-nor—meaning not one thing is able to separate us from the love of God that is in Christ Jesus our Lord (vv. 38, 39).

40 First John 4:18a. Compare with 2 Timothy 1:7.

41 First John 4:17. Love has matured in the believer when fear is replaced by boldness in anticipation of standing before the Almighty. Our union with God makes us alienated from this world but at home where God Himself dwells. See also 1 John 2:28.

42 First John 4:18b. One interesting note from the Greek language here lies in the word *ballo*, which means to throw. *Ballo* is an old word, implying that God's love does not simply sweep fear aside, but it hurls it away with speed and force. Truly, love is the demise of dread.

43 Second Timothy 1:7. See note 1, chapter 3.

44 There are both communicable and incommunicable qualities of God's nature that, through revelation, are intended to impact God's subjects and distinguish Him from all others. By incommunicable we mean those attributes of God that incite our wonder and worship of God, but

characteristics that cannot be imitated by any other (i.e., omniscience, omnipresence, omnipotence). By communicable qualities, we mean those characteristics that may be seen and known in the lives of every elect offspring of Jehovah. These family likenesses include the Spirit's fruit. See also Galatians 5:22, 23.

[45] Love's motivation, as with all Spirit fruit, flows out of obedience to God. Biblical love is never reduced to mere fickle feeling; hence, love is an activity of grace that engenders increased love when it is used and applied. See also Matthew 22:37; Philippians 4:9; 1 John 5:1–3.

[46] Ephesians 3:13. The Greek *thlipsis* (afflictions) so characterized Paul as he fulfilled his gospel ministry that he was concerned that his on-looking brethren not lose heart. Paul was a spectacle of suffering, a whipping boy for the offense of the gospel and, yet the apostle saw it rather as a glory in that it strengthened the resolve of saints every place.

[47] Second Corinthians 1:4. *Thlipsis* (Greek) is here rendered *trouble*. The kind of trouble described is any or every and covers a broad area of difficulty that Christians may face.

[48] Romans 8:29, 30. The golden chain of God's redemption or salvation is enumerated in these two verses as foreknowledge (election), predestination, effectual call, justification, and glorification. The marvelous chain of God's grace toward His own has already been accomplished by the redeeming purpose of God. The full realization of that accomplishment toward God's own is simply a matter of time.

[49] Romans 8:38, 39. The point of the apostle is plainly the utter impossibility of saints to be separated from the love of God in Christ Jesus. Should something impede or divide God's loving attachment to His own, it would mean that the golden chain is broken and God's salvific purpose toward His own failed miserably. God's nature and purpose toward His own makes this an impossibility.

[50] Psalm 23. Genuine love only seeks the highest good of others. Psalm 23 is lively to express the divine Shepherd's love toward the sheep of His fold. David reflects upon several examples of the Shepherd's loving care in his own experiences. The reflection is insightful and comforting for all sheep

belonging to Christ by the covenant of love. Can you log the specifics of the Father's love from this Psalm?

[51] "Praise the Lord," from the Hebrew, *hallelujah*. Literally, *hallelu* (praise) *yah* (Jehovah).

[52] James 2:19. Demons are said to believe (Gk., *pistos*). Believe, here, is the same Greek word used for the faith of God's elect from Titus 1:1. Obviously, demons are neither elect nor destined for the kingdom of God. What distinguishes, then, the belief of demons from the belief of saints? James labors in his letter to emphasize how the activity of faith demonstrates whether or not the faith is saving. In other words, the belief produced by the Holy Spirit results in works, in obedience, while devilish belief is dormant. Belief in God or in Jesus that does not show signs of life from above is make-believe, a pretense, or, simply stated, a false claim.

[53] Acts 8:13. Simon of Samaria is an interesting convert of the disciples. The Bible says he believed (*pistos*), was baptized, and even continued steadfastly in the disciple's company. Simon's undoing, however, lay in the fact that he wished to produce miracles like the apostles and offered them money to purchase the power of the Holy Spirit (vv. 18, 19). What follows in the narrative is somber, as Peter condemns Simon together with his money. Luke's use of the Greek word rendered *perish* is without question a term meaning damnation (v. 20). With what Peter further says of Simon (vv. 21–23), it is unlikely Simon of Samaria was a regenerate man. He may have been a convert of the apostles, but Simon evidently did not possess the transformed life produced by the Holy Spirit. Simon was a still born believer.

[54] Titus 1:1. This verse is a stellar Scripture that lucidly divides salvific faith from the superficial attachment of easy belief professions. Literally, Paul tells his readers that the faith belonging to God's elect embraces the knowledge of the truth that attends to, or is in accord with godliness. You can't cut it any clearer. Paul never advocates a works salvation, rather he teaches emphatically a salvation that works!

[55] Ephesians 2:10. God's effectual grace delivers the soul through or by means of faith, apart from works. Deliverance is a gift of grace since God justifies through faith alone and thus negates any boast of human

effort or merit (vv. 8, 9). The immediate verse speaks to those works that justifying faith produce. Again, good works flow out of the transformation of grace, but do not, in themselves, attract God's saving/justifying favor. Theologically, Ephesians 2:8, 9 addresses the justification aspect of the sinner's deliverance, while verse 10 addresses the sanctification aspect of the believer's salvation.

56 Matthew 7:20. Jesus' words are self-evident and cannot be understood as anything other than fruit inspection being the acid test of faith.

57 Philippians 2:12, 13. See notes 20 and 21, chapter 4.

58 Second Timothy 2:21. When a verse of Scripture begins with "therefore," the reader must ask himself, "What is the *therefore* there for?" In this case, the one cleansed and made fit for service to Christ is the one whose surrendered life is precious metal to God's discerning eye. The contrast of wood and clay speak to God's assessment of nominalism. These elements are contrasting lifestyles—honorable versus dishonorable (v. 20).

59 Second Timothy 3:16. If Scripture comes to us by the breath of God (Gk., *theopneustos*), then logic itself should applaud its singular sufficiency in the lives of trusting saints. Verse 17 teaches how God's Word alone is able to mature and equip believers for every useful service to God.

60 First Thessalonians 5:17. A common term for prayer of all sorts is the rendering at hand. The text assumes a continued ministry of intercessions, supplications, praise, and worship. These should become and adorn the believer's prayer life with the Father.

61 Hebrews 10:24, 25. Local church assembly is both a blessing and command to God's people. Regular assembly is implied especially in those times leading up to Christ's return. The purpose for faithful assembly includes the need to incite mutual love and labor inside and outside the assemblies (v. 24) and to exhort, confront, and encourage one another in the faith as the day of Christ approaches (v. 25).

In tough times the regular assembly of some will wane and be forsaken, but such a practice should never characterize obedient Christians who look with expectation to Christ's return (v. 25).

[62] Acts 2:41–49. Can you pick out the spiritual dynamics of the assembled church at Pentecost in Jerusalem? These features are several and the Holy Spirit has laid them out in such order and prominence that saints should both adhere and protect them for the building up of all New Testament assemblies.

[63] Romans 8:14. Sons of God are all those led by the Spirit of the living God. The objective telltale of true believers lies in their manifest conformity to the Spirit's inspired Word from God, the Bible.

[64] Genesis 32:30. The Peniel moment for Jacob was the place of his wrestling encounter with Jehovah. The Peniel moment for redeemed hearts is the place where God is likewise encountered and embraced for increased wisdom and knowledge of the Holy One.

CHAPTER 7

Practicum

Years ago, while teaching a class on biblical counseling at the college level, one of my students asked me if I was awakened during the night by the strong urge to create new counseling assignments for homework.

Yes, practicum is vital. Assignments whereby the students or clients must put into practice the things they are reading or studying is vital to retention, to learning. Even the process of inventing new and helpful ideas to assist behavioral change enables the planner, the teacher, or the counselor to change himself through practice. All who struggle with fear should be very industrious, working at new ideas and upgrading old ones to help facilitate rehabituation and change.

Currently, I am in the process of revising a 365-page devotional that I wrote many years ago, wherein I address a different problem, issue, sin, or struggle every day of the year.

Each article provides relevant Scripture, a body of practical counsel, and an assignment section. The latter section was intended for the reader to work out the application in specific, doable, concrete ways. Many have been helped by it, and Christian leaders have found it useful for quick reference when facing a presenting need. *The Daily Counselor*[1] was printed locally and distributed in the same manner. I expect soon to finish the revision so that this devotional can be published and assist people in a greater way.

In the first of the three sections belonging to this chapter, I will be using questions and assignments from this manual, which is intended both for implementation and ideas. Hopefully, this section will be useful for combat and as an incentive for further thinking and planning on behalf of you, the reader. There's just something remedial about designing one's own arsenal to strengthen oneself and others (Rom. 15:14;[2] 2 Cor. 1:4).[3]

Evaluation Questions and Remedial Assignments for Troop Preparedness

1. Presenting Issue: *Anxious Living*
   Reading Assignment: Ecclesiastes 3:1–8
   Remedial Prescription:
   For one week, record every situation that causes you anxiety, frustration, nervousness, or irritability. Become aware of your actions and how you are failing to accept God's purposes for your life. Write out a brief plan of how you can respond to life's changes in a more God-honoring way. Put your plan into action each time you are tempted to lose perspective. If you remain diligent in doing this, you will make steady progress toward peace.

2. Presenting Issue: *An Effective Worry Remover*
   Reading Assignment: Titus 3:4–7
   Remedial Prescription:
   a. Explain how the knowledge of God's infinite kindness and love is an effective worry remover.
   b. According to Titus 3:7, what did God purpose in the appearance of the incarnate Christ?

3. Presenting Issue: *Phobic Reactions*
   Reading Assignment: Job 5:8, 9
   Remedial Prescription:
   Consider the further implications of Eliphaz's counsel in Job 5:9. Discuss on paper how this thought applies to the afflictions of men (i.e., phobias). What one major factor does Eliphaz's counsel teach of which humanistic counsel is void?

4. Presenting Issue: *Fear of Man*
   Reading Assignment: Proverbs 29:23–27
   Remedial Prescription:
   a. Jot down some common faults (sins) that result from the fear of man. Consider the concessions, compromises, and crimes that are often committed when people choose to conform to social pressure.
   b. How about you? Is the fear of man keeping you from being what God wants you to be for Him? Repent of this sin; commit Psalm 56:11 to memory as you live out your life daily in the fear of God!

5. Presenting Issue: *Lifetime Bondage*
   Reading Assignment: Hebrews 2:9–18
   Remedial Prescription:
   a. Apprehensions of death and questions about its shadow are logical considerations of thinking Christians. When thoughts of death begin to trouble us and we become frightfully aware of death and dying, something is wrong with our way of thinking. A prayerful review of the book of Romans should provide you with resources for repentance and grounds for assurance.
   b. Draw up a weekly schedule listing all of your activities, recreations, and responsibilities. Now that you have done this, share how each contributes to a wise

investment of time in light of eternity. Develop a view of life as a responsible steward with wise investments maturing beyond the grave.

6. Presenting Issue: *Sidetracked by Fear*
   Reading Assignment: Luke 21:25–28
   Remedial Prescription:
   Have you been sidetracked from the real issues of life? Read Colossians 1:23 and discuss the ways you could be subtly moved away from the gospel. Counteract Satan's distraction with biblical practices to cultivate alertness in times like these.

7. Presenting Issue: *Daily Stress Factors*
   Reading Assignment: Psalm 37:1–11
   Remedial Prescription:
   I suggest that you commit to memory the five words below. Use them today to turn stress factors into success factors! Trust (v. 3); Delight (v. 4); Commit (v. 5); Rest (v. 7); Cease (v. 8).

8. Presenting Issue: *Dispelling Despair*
   Reading Assignment: Psalm 73
   Remedial Prescription:
   Make a list of potential feeders for despair in your life. Counteract the subtle influence of unrighteous feeders with profitable activities. Replace the old with the new. Take your first step of change as soon as possible!

9. Presenting Issue: *Overwhelmed*
   Reading Assignment: Luke 10:38–42
   Remedial Prescription:
   a. When you become overwhelmed with responsibility, it can be helpful to quietly breathe a Scripture, like that

found in Isaiah 30:15: "[I]n quietness and confidence shall be your strength." Let this or another relevant verse remind you to slow down a moment and make a sensible assessment of things. If you practice this procedure regularly, you will find it easier to handle the pressure of heavier moments.

b. Instead of looking at the size of some great and urgent responsibility, learn to prioritize the immediate needs. Apply yourself to the task just in front of you and "take no thought for the morrow; for the morrow shall take thought for the things of itself" (Matt. 6:34).

10. Presenting Issue: *Master Despondency*
Reading Assignment: Psalm 105:17–24
Remedial Prescription:
a. Read Psalm 105:19, and see the relationship between Joseph's fetters (v. 18) and God's purposes.
b. Commit Psalm 105:19 to memory, and use this verse together with prayer and Christian fellowship to confront master despondency.

11. Presenting Issue: *Bad Moods*
Reading Assignment: Psalm 84
Remedial Prescription:
a. Note the truths found in Psalm 84:4, 5, 7. Use a Bible commentary and make some notes regarding the meaning and application of these verses to you and your moods.
b. Can you list some biblical helps for combating the tendency of feeling down, or feeling self-pity when cares and routine begin to oppress? Example: Christian fellowship (Psalm 84:4a), praise (Psalm 84:4b).

12. Presenting Issue: *The Sufficient Shepherd*
    Reading Assignment: Psalm 23
    Remedial Prescription:
    a. The tendency of sheep is to turn to their own ways (Isa. 53:6). Note the provision that flows from the sheep abiding with the shepherd in Psalm 23. Ask yourself if you are honestly enjoying the benefits and perspective that God's personal fellowship affords.
    b. Should you find today that your fellowship with God has become stale, turn back to Him. In earnest confession of your self-willed ways, take the matter of your wanderings to the Shepherd. Make a practice of reading this psalm regularly until its message is a personal reality in your daily life. Let Psalm 23 always be your reminder to walk daily in the Shepherd's sufficiency.

13. Presenting Issue: *Reliance Upon God*
    Reading Assignment: Psalm 20
    Remedial Prescription:
    a. What practical lessons do we learn from Psalm 20 as it relates to the contemporary message of medical science and psychotropic drug therapy?
    b. What precautions do you need to take when evaluating your own inner struggles?

14. Presenting Issue: *More Grace*
    Reading Assignment: Philippians 2:1–11
    Remedial Prescription:
    a. Use your Bible concordance to study out the negative dividends of pride in your life.
    b. Repent of the pride you detect in your life and follow specific practices of humility for a solution to your problem. (Example: Desire for public attention and

recognition [pride]. Give unselfishly and anonymously to another's need [humility]. Additional Scripture: 3 John 9; cp Matt. 6:3, 4. c.) List specific sinful habits in your life. Surrender anew to further commitments of yieldedness. Don't give up. Stick with it! Fear of failure is pride, whereas humility constantly trusts God for His grace.

15. Presenting Issue: *Love Him Truly*
    Reading Assignment: John 21:15–17
    Remedial Prescription:
    What situation or event has Jesus put into your life recently that calls upon your answer to the question of John 21:15? Don't delay that decision; rather, make it now—for Jesus' sake. Record it, sign it, and date it. Let your supreme devotion to Jesus be a no debated issue.

16. Presenting Issue: *The Mighty Counselor*
    Reading Assignment: Isaiah 40:12–26
    Remedial Prescription:
    Spend some time in the meditation of this text today. Record further insights you glean from the contemplation of God's greatness. Whatever your problems or the problem of those God brings your way, always be aware of the greatness of God to meet the need as you call upon Him.

17. Presenting Issue: *Planning for Lordship*
    Reading Assignment: Matthew 3:13–17; Philippians 2:3
    Remedial Prescription:
    a. Write out clear goals for yourself in relation to your Christian maturity.
    b. What are the particular obstacles you are facing that keep you from realizing your spiritual growth objectives?

    c. Contemplate possible solutions to the obstacles facing you by seeking godly counsel, by personal study, and through resultant creativity. You will need to carefully schedule changes in the areas of your difficulties. Significant progress can be made in your problem areas as you schedule, stick with your schedule, and make yourself accountable to others for your change.

18. Presenting Issue: *Strong Confidence*
    Reading Assignment: Proverbs 3:19–26
    Remedial Prescription:
    a. Whenever you face problems, remember that you are the crowning act of God's creation. This knowledge requires that you must always look beyond the material to God.
    b. Govern all that you say and do with the perspective of your position in God's plan.

19. Presenting Issue: *Sustaining Faith*
    Reading Assignment: Genesis 50:22–26; Hebrews 11:22
    Remedial Prescription:
    Search out some special promises of God that apply to you as a Christian. Begin to engraft these promises into your heart by meditation and memorization. Remember, Joseph's ability to trust God was vitally connected to his ability to recall God's promises.

20. Presenting Issue: *Change Factors*
    Reading Assignment: 2 Corinthians 3:18–4:1
    Remedial Prescription:
    List any misconceptions that our world embraces concerning change and misconceptions you may have held that seem foreign to Scripture's teaching. Can you

discern them biblically? Share how today's lesson gives you increased hope for seeing measurable growth.

21. Presenting Issue: *Seeing Conflicts God's Way*
    Reading Assignment: Galatians 5:16, 25; Romans 8:5
    Remedial Prescription:
    a. Take a few moments and memorize the nine spirit fruits. Practice today drawing upon these inner qualities of grace when you are faced with a conflict. Remember to be specific in your exercise of God's viewpoint.
    b. Share today's counsel with a Christian friend and compare notes on your mutual growth in seeing conflicts God's way.

22. Presenting Issue: *Setting Your Heart in Order*
    Reading Assignment: 1 Corinthians 11:34, 14:40; Titus 1:5
    Remedial Prescription:
    a. On paper, identify a specific sin in your life that you know needs to be confessed and repented of. Be completely honest and candid.
    b. Each time this problem occurs, make it a point to follow this procedure:
        First: Write out the specific circumstance that led to your sinful attitude or action (what happened?).
        Second: Using Scripture, describe the nature of your offense against God and man (what sin was committed?).
        Third: Explain how you could have handled the situation in a God-honoring way (what did God require?).
        Fourth: List further steps God would have you take to make adequate restitution (what does God require now?).

Fifth: Prepare yourself for battle by committing to memory a verse that you find helpful (what is my defense?).

   c. It might be best to abbreviate and memorize the above steps so that these may be automatically employed when you face that certain sin. The important thing is to continually confront your sin and upon confession immediately follow a definite course of action for change. If you keep with it and if your heart is toward Christ, you will make the desired change in time!

23. Presenting Issue: *Your Commitment to Jesus*
    Reading Assignment: Revelation 3:1–6
    Remedial Prescription:
    a. Write out exactly how you are committed to make your relationship with Jesus successful. Share definite areas and instances of your increased watchfulness.
    b. Our relationship with the Savior becomes successful when, as in the marriage relationship, we sincerely commit ourselves to that relationship. Are you sincerely committed to Jesus? If so, then "strengthen that which remains." What further actions do you need to take in order to strengthen your commitment to Christ?

24. Presenting Issue: *Maintain Good Works*
    Reading Assignment: Titus 3:8
    Remedial Prescription:
    a. Using Philippians 2:12, 13 and Ephesians 2:8–10, discuss how the maintenance of good works and godly living fit into God's plan for our lives.
    b. List some practical incentives that arise from the fact that we are compelled to maintain good works.
    c. Define and meditate upon the word *careful* as found in

our Titus text. How does the use of this word help you to understand your duty of obedience more fully?

25. Presenting Issue: *Conquering Those Obstacles*
    Reading Assignment: 1 Samuel 17:1–11
    Remedial Prescription:
    a. Whatever serious problems or great difficulties you may face today, don't be fearful! Begin to plan how you will tackle the obstacles with the resources God has supplied. Venture forth. Don't shrink back!
    b. Choose one verse on trust or faith to claim for today. Before this day is over, record specific instances where you acted upon the Scripture you selected. Make a practice of trusting the Lord!

26. Presenting Issue: *Unhooked and Reprogrammed*
    Reading Assignment: 1 Corinthians 6:9–11
    Remedial Prescription:
    Whatever sinful habits dominate one's life, the solution is only found in Christ. To break with sin and the destructive habits of the flesh, one must:
    a. Come to personal, saving faith in Jesus Christ (John 1:12—Regeneration).
    b. Restructure one's total way of living. Former sinful practices must be replaced by new, holy practices (Eph. 4:22–44—Repentance).
    c. Cultivate a daily yieldedness to Christ and endeavor to obey all that God requires of you in His Word (Rom. 6:13—Reliance).

27. Presenting Issue: *Fruitful Evidence*
    Reading Assignment: 2 Peter 1:1–8
    Remedial Prescription:
    Carefully examine the negative qualities of your life that

need continued improvement. Purpose to put off each negative quality with a positive counterpart. Trust that God will enable you to make continued change in your life for His glory as you persevere in obedient practice (Phil. 1:12, 13).

28. Presenting Issue: *Confronting Slothfulness*
    Reading Assignment: Proverbs 6:6–11
    Remedial Prescription:
    a. Do a little study on the ant. Write down as many practical lessons on diligence and industry as you can find. Apply them!
    b. Discern where you tend to be slothful in your Christian life. Set some goals for yourself in these areas and exercise diligence in following the example of our friend, the ant.

29. Presenting Issue: *In Control*
    Reading Assignment: Proverbs 25:28
    Remedial Prescription:
    List on a sheet of paper all events and activities in which you participate and occupy yourself. Go back over the list and indicate with a plus or minus whether or not these things are profitable to your Christian life. Plan to replace unprofitable activities with creative, biblical alternatives. You can do this exercise in regard to attitudes, actions, and habits alike.

30. Presenting Issue: *My Big Problem*
    Reading Assignment: 1 Corinthians 10:1–5
    Remedial Prescription:
    a. Do you feel disadvantaged in making gains against some big problem in your Christian experience? Measure up

your biblical resources against the problem, and then answer the question of Romans 8:31.
b. Confess to God your unwillingness to handle the problem. Begin to recommit yourself to working at a biblical solution for growth amid the problem. Understanding your past life and present vulnerabilities is important, but remember, God has *freed* you to appropriate His truths through a quickened spirit and a new life!

31. Presenting Issue: *Can't Quit*
Reading Assignment: 1 Thessalonians 5:16–24
Remedial Prescription:
a. Contemplate what would happen in your life if you were to give up the good fight of faith. Consider the implications to your own mind and heart and the impact it would have on those about you.
b. List biblical ways you would handle a difficulty or sin in your life that seems to be continually defeating you. Use your mind and write out sound means by which you can deal with dominating sin! (Consider the resources God has given you.)

32. Presenting Issue: *Biblical Motivation*
Reading Assignment: 1 Peter 2:11–19
Remedial Prescription:
a. Seek to relate biblical incentives for changes you would like to make in your life.
b. Ponder biblical reasons why this day in your life is so worthwhile.

33. Presenting Issue: *Bible Benefits and Blessings*
    Reading Assignment: Psalm 119:121–128
    Remedial Prescription:
    The following Scriptures give testimony to the benefits and blessings of the Bible. In brief, summarize the benefit next to the appropriate Scripture:
    Hebrews 4:12
    Psalm 119:105, 130
    Ephesians 5:26
    Joshua 1:8
    Acts 20:32
    Psalm 119:11
    Psalm 19:7–11
    John 17:17
    2 Peter 1:3, 4
    2 Timothy 3:16

34. Presenting Issue: *Set Apart*
    Reading Assignment: Deuteronomy 7:1–6
    Remedial Prescription:
    a. Here are several portions of Scripture related to our calling as holy people unto the Lord. Read the following texts and write a brief statement beside each, expressing the basic teaching of that verse: Titus 1:1; Romans 3:20; Ephesians 2:8–10; Galatians 5:22–25; Hebrews 10:39; Romans 6:4; Titus 3:8; Colossians 3:1–3; 1 Thessalonians 5:22; Romans 12:12; 1 John 1:7; Titus 2:11–14.
    b. Honestly confront areas of your life where you have allowed the world to creep in. Identify the effects these concessions have had, or will have upon you and your loved ones. Confess your sin and begin today to lift up a holy standard in obedience to your calling of grace.

35. Presenting Issue: *Appointed to Affliction*
    Reading Assignment: 1 Thessalonians 3:1–5
    Remedial Prescription:
    a. Christ has commanded each one of us to disciple men. Whatever your place of service for Him, include the message of suffering as an essential part of the gospel you teach.
    b. How do you handle the tribulations of life? Renew your perspective of the Christian gospel by engrafting First Thessalonians 3:3 to your heart and mind and by making the daily commitment to handle life's deepest valleys in ways that will please God most. A daily diary can help you become personally accountable for your maturity.

36. Presenting Issue: *Joy Made Full*
    Reading Assignment: John 15:11
    Remedial Prescription:
    a. Endeavor today to replace every gloomy thought with Scripture. It would be best to compile a list of blessings that you can use as spiritual ammunition.
    b. Focus on becoming like Christ in each and every part of your daily routine.
    c. Confess and forsake negative emotional reactions, and then share a positive spirit that speaks of hope and joy.

37. Presenting Issue: *Perfect Peace*
    Reading Assignment: Philippians 4:4–9
    Remedial Prescription:
    a. Plan in this day to confront worry or anxiety with sincere prayer on every hand.
    b. Write out a Scripture verse that you will use today to replace thoughts of worry.

c. Fill mental loitering (idleness) with useful activity. Praise the Lord for today's blessings as you retire from the day's labor.

38. Presenting Issue: *The Price of Impatience*
    Reading Assignment: Genesis 29:15–20
    Remedial Prescription:
    a. List specific examples of impatience in your life. Consider the example you are setting before your children and others looking on. Make a choice to manifest more control over your natural impulses and seek specific opportunities to use patience in edifying those who look to your example.
    b. Do a family devotional on the subject of patience, or waiting on God. Gather input from family members on ways and means of demonstrating patience in their daily lives. Determine as a family to communicate and cultivate patience as would please Christ.

39. Presenting Issue: *Healing and Health*
    Reading Assignment: Exodus 15:22
    Remedial Prescription:
    a. Are you keeping your healing and health in biblical perspective? Write out several ways your body can serve you to fulfill the ministry objectives of Philippians 1:20.
    b. Complete a weekly Christian service chart. Include everything that you would consider a service to Jesus: visitation, writing edifying letters, ministering phone calls, Bible Studies, praying for others, youth work, Bible clubs, hospitality, helping people in practical ways, nursery, etc. Consider the measure of your involvement by calculating the approximate time you spend in these tasks. Use this chart to motivate your body, soul, and spirit to faithful engagement in fruitful service.

40. Presenting Issue: *Spiritual Rebirth*
    Reading Assignment: John 3:1–8
    Remedial Prescription:
    The only sure foundation you have of spiritual rebirth lies in the premise and promise of Holy Scripture. List the biblical assurances you have of God's transforming work of grace in your life.

Life Readiness and Every Day Rehab Strategies

This next section of our practicum will focus on varied helps and rehab samplings that have strengthened others (and me) against the showdown with fear. Rehearsing the forthcoming strategy gives the combatant a certain edge over the unexpected. Someone has said that to be caught without a plan is, in itself, a sure plan for defeat (1 Pet. 5:8).[4]

First: Lean heavily upon the names and nature of the true and living God every day! *Know His Name.* Each and every day, ponder a specific name of God and write down what the name means to you for the day at hand. Ask yourself how God reveals Himself to you by the name He declares Himself to be today!

What's in a Name?
Jehovah: Self-Existent One (Ex 3:14)
Elohim: The Strong One (Gen 1:26)
Adonai: Sovereign Master (Ex 34:23)
El-Elyon: Strongest Strong One (Isa 14:13, 14)
El-Roi: Strong One Who Sees (Gen 16:13)
El-Shaddai: Almighty God (Gen 17:1–20)
El-Olam: Everlasting God (Isa 40:28)
Jehovah Jireh: The God Who Provides (Gen 22:13, 14)
Jehovah Nissi: Lord My Banner (Ex 17:15)
Jehovah Shalom: Lord Our Peace (Jdg 6:24)
Jehovah Sabboath: Lord of Hosts (1 Sam 1:3)

Jehovah Raah: Lord My Shepherd (Ps 23:1)
Jehovah Nakeh: God Who Judges (Ezk 7:9)
Jehovah Shammah: God Who Is Present (Ezk 48:35)

Second: Devotional protocol—*Know His Heart*
Scripture Meditation: Psalm 119:113–120
Definition of Devotions: Maintaining private or personal devotions has to do with cultivating, by the means of personal prayer and Bible study, increased love and loyalty to God.

1. The Need of Personal Devotions
   a. Apparent from Bible commands: 2 Titus 2:15; 2 Peter 3:18; Colossians 3:16.
   b. Apparent from biblical illustrations: Joshua 1:8—Joshua; Psalm 119:2—David; Genesis 24:63—Isaac; Genesis 5:22—Enoch; Mark 1:35—Jesus.

2. The Time for Personal Devotions
   Scripture does not exact a specific time for personal devotions, only that both day and night are seasonable for meditation.
   a. The psalmist said, "Early will I seek Thee" (Ps 63:1).
   b. Isaac "went into the fields at eventide to meditate" (Gen 24:63).
   Godly believers such as Spurgeon, Edwards, Hamm, and Mueller would not so much as begin a day's activities without spending sufficient time with the Master.
   The important thing to remember about devotions is that it must be a time of solitude when the door of care is shut—a time long enough to leave His sweet fragrance upon our hearts throughout our daily activity.

3. The Objectives of Personal Devotions
   a. To increase our love for Christ. If our private devotions

do not result in this, then we are going through a merely mechanical exercise!
   b. To know Christ's leading (Ps 119: 105).
   c. To rise above temptation (Ps 119:11).
   d. To grow in grace through spiritual exercise (1 Tim 4:8, 15).

Practice makes perfect; likewise, the Christian's spiritual maturity rises only to the extent that he has been exercised in God's Word (1 Tim 4:7).

Nourishing Exercise:
1. Work through the outline above, looking up all corresponding Scripture.
2. Fold a sheet of paper into three equal parts, lengthwise. At the top of the paper, beginning at the far left, write *Scripture*. In the middle, write *Meaning*. At the top of the right column, write *Application*. Use this procedure to record your Scripture study notes as you search the Word daily in regular devotions.

Third: Pray like Daniel—*Know God's mind*
Scripture Meditation: Daniel 9:1–19

No question about it, Daniel was a man who was mighty with God and with men. Born of royal blood, possibly of the house of Hezekiah, Daniel was fervent toward God from his youth. The fervent spirit of Daniel is especially seen in his prayer life. Prayer was paramount in Daniel's life. His commitment to pray nearly cost Daniel his life (Dan 6), but this was of little consequence to this spiritual prince. Daniel's communion with God took precedence over everything else.

The preeminence of prayer in the life of Daniel is best illustrated in today's Scripture meditation. Daniel understood Jeremiah's prophecy of seventy years, and he knew full well that the captivity of Judah was coming to an end. In view of this, and in an earnest attempt to turn the heart of God to look upon a rebellious people with renewed favor, Daniel seeks the Lord in prayer. Few prayers in the Bible allow us to peer into the very heart of a man like the one before us. Let's examine Daniel's prayer with a receptive heart.

1. Using Daniel 9:3, list how Daniel prepared himself to seek the God of heaven in prayer.
2. Work through Daniel's prayer carefully and write down the particular characteristics of his prayer that seem outstanding to you. An example might be: Daniel is concerned for God's holiness.
3. Discuss briefly what you perceive to be the nature of Daniel's prayer. What do you see as his leading petition?

Although Daniel was among the holiest men of his day, how is it apparent that Daniel identifies himself alongside the rebellious children of Israel? Cite specific Scripture verses with your answer.

According to Daniel 9:20, 21, at what time was the angel Gabriel sent forth from God to answer Daniel's supplication?

It's little wonder that Daniel could rebuke the king before "a thousand of his lords" (Dan 5:1), stop the mouths of bloodthirsty lions, and remain calm through it all! Daniel stood on firm praying ground and prevailed with the Ruler of heaven and earth!

Remedial Prescription

Is your life plagued with fears and anxieties? Do you lack enablement to overcome sinful habits? Does your service for Christ seem rather ineffective to meet real needs in the lives of others? Set your heart and mind to prayer. Devise a daily prayer schedule and stick with it. Establish an agenda for prayer and make yourself accountable to someone. Record your decision to follow Daniel's example today.

Fourth: Pursue lifelong rules of engagement—*Know His zeal* (Jn 2:7).[5]
Use alliteration, acrostic, or lyrical style formulas that will

enable you to quickly remember life preparedness and battle strategies for any given situation. Football players must have game plans down pat. They have little time in the huddle for a chalkboard explanation. The players need to be good to go as a plan is yelled out by a blunt, abbreviated signal.

Below are the examples of two plans, the first for engaging life itself and the second, in the event I face a fear episode today.

Plan A
My life plan as a contestant of grace (i.e., W-R-E-S-T-L-E):

- Walk with God, using every legitimate means at your disposal to keep short accounts with God and man (Acts 24:16).[6]

- Rely upon God's Word as your inspired plumb line for every thought and deed. It alone is authoritative and sufficient for your life and service (Eph 6:17).[7]

- Engage the Enemy. I will, by God's strength, embrace my responsibility to fight the good fight and I will, with God's help, embrace Jesus Christ in order to subvert my fears (James 4:7).[8]

- Strategize your game—planning, writing, scheduling personal diaries, strategizing helps for others, whatever is necessary to become more Christ like! Seeing I am already enabled by God's Spirit to change for the better, I will investigate ways and means to know Christ and overcome myself (2 Col 10:5).[9]

- Testify to faith. Only changed lives will change the world; sharing my victories in God will give others hope as well as provide ongoing accountability for change within myself (2 Col 1:5).[10]

- Live joyfully. There are certain mechanics, a certain regiment to godliness. Yet in my discipline of holiness I don't want to quench the Savior's joy. Holiness is a joyful routine because my life is bound to the rails of destiny. I am freed to live joyfully because my life is on course to apprehend Jesus Christ (Ps 16:11).[11]

- Encourage the faint. Investing in others, planting seeds that transform and reform is remedial and spiritually healthy. Inciting others to grow and change brings me out of my self-absorbed ways and renews my soul by the strength that service affords (1 Th 4:18).[12]

Long ago, Jonathan Edwards compiled a lengthy list of resolves[13] that have always goaded my commitment to the Lord. Edwards had a plan, and as a result his life and writings still impact many today, although he only lived into his fifties. The same could be said of his son, Jonathan the Younger, and of that prince of preachers, Charles Spurgeon. Their years were brief, but their resolves to godliness still impact us today. The life we have received by grace is worth every effort and inconvenience to the flesh. Every grace effort is effectual.

Plan B

This is a sampling of a good personal plan to implement should I face a fear episode today:

A Biblical Blueprint for B-a-t-t-l-e:

1. Begin to give expression to your feeling by verbalizing your confidence in God. Recall the description of your God

from Psalm 61 and address Him as your Rock, your Strong Tower, your Shelter, your Covering (Ps. 61:2, 3, 4).

2. Aspire to God for deliverance through confession of your frustration and all known sin. Tell the Lord exactly what is going on inside your heart. Be completely open and honest with the Lord (Ps. 61:2).

3. Trust the promises of God by rehearsing them aloud and by crying out to God to meet you in your place of need. Be expressive and intense; let the tears flow and cast your burden upon the Lord (Ps. 61:2, 5–7).

4. Tune your heart God-ward by singing His praises. Rejoice in Him, and utilize the vehicle of music to express your pleas to God and to replace the discord within your heart (Ps. 61:8).

5. Look for God-given opportunities to give the Lord what is due Him through the faithful performance of His will. Look for ways and means to assume your biblical responsibility to serve God and others. Practice what you know is right and needful daily (Ps. 61:8).

6. Engage the obstacle at hand with an unflinching resolve to be an overcomer. Refuse every easy way out that discounts confidence in the Captain. "Pay your vows day after day ..." (Ps. 61:8).

Remedial Prescription:
1. Get hold of a church hymnal and select some songs that you can employ as you engage in singing the praises of God. Choose hymns that speak of God's nature and greatness. List them in your journal.

2. Don't keep this blueprint to yourself! In your notebook, list the names of people who may be going through a valley in their Christian experience. Purpose to share Psalm 61 with the

---

Chapter Seven Endnotes

[1] Mark L. Graham, *The Daily Counselor* (set) (Interlaken, NY: I.T. Publications of Interlaken, 1989).

[2] Romans 15:14. The apostle is commending his readers regarding the maturity of their Christian walk. The Roman saints were demonstrating by their lives a stellar quality of Christian virtue and insight, together with a notable skill in biblical counseling, "Able also to admonish [*nouthete o*] one another." The ability to effectually admonish others is a nurtured quality that finds its success through the power of the Holy Spirit (v. 13).

[3] Second Corinthians 1:4. See note 45, chapter 6, remembering the application of comfort is intended to be actualized for one and all.

[4] First Peter 5:8. To be sure, the adversary of saints is quite sober and vigilant in his intention to derail their faith. What is therefore admonished in the text is nothing short of serious industry on behalf of believers as they engage life and a lurking foe.

[5] John 2:7. Jesus had a plan to manifest the Father's glory wherever He went. His zeal for a glorious outcome never found Him in want of strategy.

[6] Acts 24:16. A self-evident goal on short accounts from the heart of Paul.

[7] Ephesians 6:17. It appears that the sword of the Spirit is so described here that the reader might know with certainty that the Bible is intended for tactical aggression. It is sufficient to subdue every lethal threat to one's faith.

[8] James 4:7. See note 12, chapter 4.

9 Second Corinthians 10:5. See note 11, chapter 4.

10 Second Corinthians 1:5. This is exactly what Paul is doing in the verse before us! By sharing the consolations of Christ in his own sufferings, the suffering Corinthians also found the sweet consolations of Jesus through Paul's example and teaching.

11 Psalm 16:11. The passage is very messianic, yet the application is true for us. Life, joy, and pleasures forevermore are the assurance, while predestination is the plan. I'm on the glory road, and nothing is able to dissuade that promised certainty (Rom 8:28 ff). Daily, I am freed to reckon with this reality, despite the daunting obstacles.

12 First Thessalonians 4:18. An imperative and an antidote for my self-defeating faint heartedness (i.e., "Comfort one another with these words"). Now that's inspired comfort to know and to share!

13 *Jonathon Edwards' Resolutions*, ed. Stephen Nichols (Phillipsburg, NJ: P & R Publishing , 2001), internet accessed, June 25, 2013.

A Concluding Q and A Session

When writing a book of this nature, so many questions spin around in the author's heart and soul, such as:

- What are the goals and objectives of this labor and to what audience should the message of the text be directed?
- What are the issues of priority and to what extent are these things to be addressed?
- What cadence do I give to this book?

Theology is essential, readability is necessary and personal testament breeds hope by observation, so, how do I express these matters?

In short, I do not presume this work to meet the specs of all my readers. What, then, is my all consuming purpose? It is to exalt an all-sufficient Savior. Mine is yet another voice that sings of God's grace! This is the intended strength of my writing effort.

Could more be said on the subject? But of course! Could we have explored more deeply other aspects of biblical counseling which might further the healing process of the suffering? Ah, without a doubt!

Nonetheless, I have chosen to write what is sufficient for the immediate need: to engage human fear by the exercise of faith alone in Jesus Christ!

With that said, let me conclude with some candid answers to

some important questions regarding irrational fears. Such questions have surfaced often in my counseling experience and these are questions that may predicate a sequel to what I have written.

1. Q. Is irrational fear sinful behavior?

    A. We know from God's Word that fear first manifested itself when Adam's sinning resulted in his hiding from God (Gen 3:10). Irrational fear is a bizarre escalation of deceitful imaginations from the heart of man. It is both the sinful imaginations of inner depravity (testifying to man's brokenness), as well as the inner smoke of spiritual warfare filling the soul.

    The stimuli for fear is all around us. Stimuli, however, is only stimuli! The Lord intends for us to fight the temptation to fear with faith, *"for whatsoever is not of faith is sin"* (Ro 14:23). Irrational fear must first and above all else be seen for what it is: namely, faithlessness. Repentance, then, becomes the first step of harnessing sinful fallout. Again, the temptation to fear abounds all around our broken world and sin's call lies within and without, pushing and pulling at our souls continually. Nonetheless, *"where sin abounded, grace abounded much more"* (Ro 5:20).

2. Q. Is there a predisposition to irrational fear?

    A. If someone is asking about a genetic bent to sin, then I would say, yes! In fact, all humanity has a genetic bent to fear and not to faith (Ps 51:5). Practice and exercise strengthens both perfection and imperfection. Each individual has the capacity for habit and, thus, the ability to develop skill in the good, as well as the bad in fearing and in believing. It is easier to sin against God than to obey Him. Sinful disposition is at the heart of every man, but the Gospel of Jesus Christ can renew lives after His own image as enabling grace motivates the exercise of godliness (I Tim 4:7,8).

3. Q. If a mood altering drug enables a person to focus on Christ with more stability, why not use it and keep the stressors of life at bay?

   A. Remember always that the use of psychotropic medication is a coping mechanism; it is a means, a method, a manner of coping with life. The message of the mystery of redemption is *"Christ in you, the hope of glory"* (Col 1:27). Jesus Christ is intended to be the all-sufficient means of dealing successfully with troubles of the heart and soul. With this said, maturing in Christ is a life-long rigor, and with spiritual growth and maturity comes the wisdom necessary to appropriate more grace for our stressors (Ja 1:21).

4. Q. Is it always wrong to avoid the elevator and take the stairs in order to avoid the phobic struggle altogether?

   A. The point, here, that should be emphasized is this: fear should not hinder my freedom in Christ. Nothing must box me in so that I am prevented, or hindered from being and doing what God would have me be or do in any given situation. Indeed, *"I can do all things through Christ who strengthens me"* (Php 4:13).

   What this does *not* mean is that I am to be on the hunt for stressors (Mt 6:13). Simply go about your business and when you are faced with options, choose what is reasonable and expedient. Many times I have chosen the hospital stairs. There is a God honoring choice in physical exercise. When people are with me, the elevator is suited to the circumstances. I have, however, refused the stairs even when alone, when I sense the motivations of my heart are pushing and pulling me away from dependence upon Christ. It is then that it becomes necessary to exercise godly motivations and manage what otherwise might ensnare me. Watch for motivations of the heart! Motivations lie at the core of human behavior, so, *"Keep your heart with all diligence, for out of it spring the issues of life"* (Pro 4:23).

5. Q. Can certain somatic conditions exacerbate the fear episode?

   A. Yes. The spirit of man is not the only part of him which has been broken by the fall. The body has been corrupted as well. Dying is symptomatic of the direction our bodies are going throughout life (Ro 6:23). The body was intended of God to work hand and glove with the soul of man, yet many times they seem to work in the reverse; in fact, they often appear hostile toward one another.

   Obviously, a weary, broken body prevents clear mindedness (in more cases than not). Anger seems to slip out of our hearts more readily when we go without sleep, or are oppressed by pain. A thorough physical examination is always recommended when adverse behavioral patterns surface, becoming more frequent/chronic. The soma, however, is not responsible for sin. The body may exacerbate sinful behavior and accommodate the natural man, despite the desire of the mind to serve Christ (Ro 7:18-25). The truth is that the body grows weak and weary and must be attended to in order to advantage the warrior of grace (I Co 6:19,20).

6. Q. Isn't irrational fear the same as a heightened fear episode?

   A. Yes. Irrational fear is full blown fear episode. It is a wholehearted yield to the bizarre antics of unreasonable and irrational thinking and feelings, i.e., thought fueled panic. Irrational fear abandons the Spirit fruit of self-control. Irrational fear is, at the same time, abandoned hope, practical atheism, and *"futility"*, a term that Paul uses to describe the believer's mind *before* coming to Jesus Christ (Eph 4:17).

Irrational fear, then, goes beyond the norms of that which is reasonable and sensible. Once again, irrational fear is not beyond the grasp of grace, as this book has shown. Heightened fear does not mean a condition of no return, even amidst the episode itself. It is neither a condition, nor a disorder that is irreversible, genetically disposed, or only manageable by drug therapy. Heightened fear is a way of thinking that is off track with God's purpose and our sense of destination (Ro 8:29). According to the Bible, behavioral transformation is the result of mind renewal, or renewal energized by the mind marinated in the ways and works of God (Ro 12:1,2; Jn 8:32).

7. Q. Since fear is so prevalent among people, doesn't the biblical way of viewing it (as sinful) and managing it (with confrontation) incite added anxiety, or depression?

A. Biblical Christianity is all about a cure, not the distribution of band-aids. Biblical counseling focuses upon the heart where the thoughts and activities of mankind originate. It is at the level of the heart, the birthplace of all fears, that the Word of God takes aim. The Word of God pierces, discerns and divides human motivations, each intention and every thought (He 4:12).

The piercing of God's Word is not comfortable to the soul of man, but like a scalpel in the hands of a wise surgeon, the truth severs all spiritual malignancy and engrafts anew the roots of righteousness. What is so precious about the power of truth is the ability it has to transform a life from the roots to the fruits. True Christ like character is the certain expectation of the fearful when the Holy Spirit is given free reign in an open heart encounter with God (II Co 3:17,18).

8. Q. What about the unbelieving who struggle with fear? How should these be approached who look to Christians for help?

   A. All true Bible based counseling is pre-counseling when it comes to helping those without Jesus Christ. Apart from the clear-cut presentation of our Lord's atonement for sin and His call to repentance and faith, our counsel simply skirts the core issue of life and forfeits spiritual healing.

   I may venture forth in a discussion of strategy with an unbelieving person, but only to demonstrate the unique process of change afforded to those in Christ. To give an assignment for change without beginning God's way through the Gospel is little more than behavior modification wrapped in Christian veneer. This may appear to be biblical counseling, but it remains humanistic without the core dynamic of a living Savior.

9. Q. Irrational fear appears on the rise in our culture; will this trend continue and how will it affect human society tomorrow?

   A. Human fear is epidemic. Even among professing Christians, chronic fear is widespread. Psychiatric medication flows in abundance and is readily accessible. The U.S. Mental Health Care Budget is exploding and the Bible speaks of this trend prophetically. Jesus Himself spoke of a coming day when men will increasingly suffer coronaries due to fear, fear of *"those things which are coming on the earth"*(Lk 21:26). Fear and coronaries! They seem to characterize faithless men and women of the latter days. Fear is symptomatic of a people who do not trust in the living God. A people so caught up in themselves that when their self-made world crumbles, their hearts fail. They become swallowed up in the abyss of their own emptiness and self-hope. The prospect for the future is not a healthy one for human society, but the Good News has never been brighter for those who sincerely long to be healed (Rev 22:17).

10. Q. In frank honesty, isn't fear management a distant cry from fear deliverance? Isn't it the intention of God to make us completely whole and miraculously healed from all fear?

A. The grace of Christ is well able to deliver redeemed hearts from each and every fear. This side of heaven, however, temptation lurks, the stimuli for fear abounds and the proneness to sin in this flesh has not been fully eradicated. The admonition to obedience and to faith is the constant theme of Holy Scripture. Maturity is measured by the experience of making right choices. These truths the Bible affirms over and over again. Indeed, there is deliverance for every fear, but as long as we live in temples of clay, there will be battles which must be fought and won in our hearts.

The stature of faith we have gained by experience is not forfeited by our occasional faltering and seasonal defeats. *"Steady now, steady as we go, easy, easy..."* is the voice of one whose hands know how to reign in a team of anxious horses. This is both management and wisdom. It is evident from the teachings of Scripture that God intends His people to learn the skill of harnessing the harassment of human fears with the wisdom and strength that He alone provides. Herein, is true deliverance in the wise management of our fears (He 5:14).

Don't focus on the miraculous to the detriment of maturity. Learn the drill and adorn those inner qualities of grace (II Co 7:1).

*"Now, may the God of peace himself
sanctify you completely, and may your
whole spirit, soul, and body be preserved
blameless at the coming of our Lord Jesus Christ."*

-First Thessalonians 5:23

Some Enduring Resources

My last input here has to do with resources. I don't intend them to be exhaustive. These resources are helpful in your ongoing pursuit of change into Christ likeness, though I am not suggesting that everything listed is necessarily without defect. There is only one reading source I know to be impeccable. The list, together with a short summary, is provided by my wife, Diane and me, together with the efforts of our friends and colleagues in the gospel, Pastor Dan and Charlotte Bunge. The summaries come largely from the aforementioned and some from published briefs. Several of these materials have made an impact on me in a way that has helped strengthen my pursuit of God by seeing life's struggles more clearly through a biblical lens.

Adams, Jay. *Christ and Your Problems*, Phillipsburg, NJ: P & R Publishing.

> Do you have problems that seem too great to bear? Do you wonder if there is any way out of the mess you are in? This helpful booklet was written to put such problem cases into perspective, showing first that no one's problems are unique. Jay Adams offers genuine hope based on God's promise in First Corinthians 10:13. Readers will gain the courage needed to take responsible action, knowing that a real solution is to be found in God's way.

—. *The Christian Counselor's Manual,* Phillipsburg, NJ: P & R Publishing, 1973.
This book deals with nouthetic counseling and addresses such things as presuppositions and principles, the practice and the process. This is a good reference book and it a must-have for any biblical counselor.

—. *Competent to Counsel,* Grand Rapids, MI: Zondervan, 1972.
Dr. Adams laid the basis for the reemergence of biblical counseling (nouthetic counseling). He sets the case for using biblical principles versus psychoanalysis in counseling Christians. Using biblically directed discussion, nouthetic counseling works by means of the Holy Spirit to bring about change in the personality and behavior of the counselee. Says Adams, *"There have been dramatic results ... not only have people's immediate problems been resolved, but there have also been solutions to all sorts of long-term problems as well."*

—. *From Forgiven to Forgiving,* Amityville, NY: Calvary Press, 1994.
When you've been wronged, the best thing to do is forgive and forget, right? That's what many Christians believe, but is it biblical? Adams dispels misconceptions about forgiveness, reveals God's true plan for absolution, and shows you how to apply it to your own relationships. Learn how to forgive and forget God's way.

—. *Godliness Through Discipline,* Phillipsburg, NJ: P & R Publishing.
Here is a practical booklet for anyone who wants to become a godlier person. In it, Adams shows clearly that, while there is no such thing as instant godliness, genuine and lasting holiness is indeed possible. Beginning with Paul's instruction in First Timothy 4:7, *"You must discipline yourself for the purpose of godliness,"* Adams explains how godly living can become second nature for the person who truly desires to be Christ like.

Anyabwile, Thabiti. *What Is a Healthy Church Member?* Wheaton, IL: Crossway, 2008.

> This little gem is a Nine Marks book and a solid biblical summary on New Testament church membership; an inspirational book for serious Christian soldiers.

Berg, Jim. *Changed into His Image: God's Plan for Transforming Your Life*, Greenville, SC: BJU Press.

> Berg has written a very sound and practical book on understanding biblical change. The subtitle, *God's Plan for Changing Your Life*, expresses well the content of this excellent study.

Biblical Counseling Foundation. *Self-Confrontation: A Manual for In-Depth Discipleship*, Palm Desert, CA.

> By helping you experience victory and contentment in all of life's difficulties and by approaching relationships and circumstances from a biblical perspective, this book will also prepare you to help others face, deal with, and endure life's deepest problems biblically.

Boston, Thomas. *The Art of Manfishing*, Christian Focus Publications, 1998.

> This is truly a Puritan's view of evangelism. First published in 1793, Boston's "scribble" enables the reader to see the duty and art of winning the lost to Jesus Christ. Human nature is so vividly explained and illustrated in this little read from a fine scholar of God's Word.

Bridges, Jerry. *Trusting God, Even When it Hurts*, Colorado Springs: Nave Press, 1988.

> Do you find it easy to trust God—until adversity strikes? When life clouds over, do you suddenly begin to suspect that you only *imagined* His care for you? Bridges uncovers three essential truths about God: He is completely sovereign, He is infinite in wisdom, and He is perfect in love. Building on these three

rocks, Bridges shows how we can learn to trust God, even when we don't understand what He is doing.

Eareckson-Tada, Joni, and Steve Estes. *When God Weeps,* Grand Rapids, MI: Zondervan Publishing House, 1997.
Joni, a quadriplegic for forty plus years after a neck injury in a diving accident as a teenager, shares these words: *"This book is not so much truths about suffering as it is about [truths of] God ... not so much about affliction as it is about the only One who can unlock sense out of suffering ... it's Steve's and my prayer that through this book you will better understand why our weeping matters to a loving God. A God who will, one day, make clear the meaning behind every tear."*

Fitzpatrick, Elyse. *Idols of the Heart: Learning to Long for God Alone,* Phillipsburg, NJ: P & R Publishers, 2001.
This book reveals that idolatry lies at the heart of every besetting sin. If you think of idols as stone statues in far-off lands, think again. Idols are the desires, longings, and expectations we worship instead of the true God. Fitzpatrick helps uncover hidden idols by moving us to ask ourselves, *"What do I long for so much that my heart demands, 'give me this, lest I die?' What must I have for my life to be meaningful and happy?"*

——. *A Steadfast Heart,* Phillipsburg, NY: P & R Publishing, 2006.
Although never our personal choice, it is frequently God's plan that His children walk through storms and difficulties. Using the picture presented in Psalm 57, you can discover the secret of experiencing God's presence and comfort in trials as you grow in your appreciation of His purposes in your life.

Halla, James. *The Plight of Fallen Man,* Stanley, NC: Timeless Texts, 2002.
Here is a book by a physician who is also a counselor. He

emphasizes that there is more to pain than just getting rid of it. There is a biblical response to pain that the believer must be made aware.

Hurding, Roger. *The Tree of Healing*, Zondervan Publishing House. Over the years, I (Mark Graham) have found Hurding's work quite helpful in discerning secular psychologies and in thinking through a Christian response to the contemporary humanistic counseling schools. Hurding also fleshes out several Christian counseling models, including nouthetic counseling, which I find to be insightful but challenging. The challenge for me with Hurding's book (and similar Christian counseling resources) lies in the rigor of good discernment. A case in point can be found in Hurding's affirmation of Richard Lovelace's words, *"Biblical truth is not a compendium of all necessary knowledge"* (p. 306). In my mind, something in Lovelace's (and Hurding's) view sounds deficient and humanistic without the fuller explanation of an all-sufficient Word from God. This reading, though insightful, begs the good exercise of keen perception and spiritual awareness.

James, Carolyn. *When Life and Beliefs Collide: How Knowing God Makes a Difference*, Grand Rapids, MI: Zondervan.
If you are a Christian woman, is your theology found in Mary *and* Martha? Thinking *and* doing? James weaves together stories of contemporary and biblical women, examining the practical benefits of knowing God deeply—and the misperceptions that discourage you from truly knowing Him. A must-read for women and highly recommended for men!

Kuen, Alfred. *I Will Build My Church,* Moody Press.
This is a good study of the church from a nonconformist view. The reading will especially profit those who dare to resist empty institutionalism and tradition while resolving to

strengthen Christ's church after a biblical pattern. Although I (Mark Graham) do not give a blanket endorsement of Kuen's theology and ideas, the book has inspired conviction for radical obedience when it comes to biblical church life.

Mack, Wayne. *Anger and Stress Management*, Merrick, NY: Calvary Press Publishing, 2004.

Dr. Wayne Mack tells you not just how to handle anger but also how to handle the root causes of anger. By doing this, Dr. Mack helps you to better understand why your reactions to stress and its accompanying anger are usually the result of not getting what you *think* you need. He then goes on to explain how to restructure your thinking to make your reaction more Christ like. If you've ever struggled with anger, if you've ever been so stressed out that you don't know where to turn then this book, saturated with Scriptural principles, can change your life—forever!

——. *Life in the Father's House,* Phillipsburg, NJ: P & R Publishing, 1996.

Ideal for new Christians and discipleship groups, this helpful book explains why joining a local Christian fellowship is essential to the spiritual health of every believer. Mack and Swavely's practical discussions on the traits of a good fellowship, leadership, male and female roles, worship, and more provide an excellent Scripturally based overview of the importance of the local Christian community.

——. *Out of the Blues: Dealing with the Blues of Depression and Loneliness,* Focus Publishing.

This book addresses the issue of depression, a problem that nearly everyone faces at some time in his or her life. Using a distinctly biblical perspective, the author defines what depression is and outlines causes and solutions to the blues caused by loneliness. It includes a Q and A section and additional notes written for counselors, making this a good resource for both those who are seeking help, and those offering help.

Mahanaey, C. J. *The Cross-Centered Life*, Colorado Springs, CO: Multnomah Books, 2002.

This read shows us how to center *every day* on the cross of Calvary and how to escape the pitfalls of legalism, condemnation, and feelings-driven faith. Keep Jesus' work on your behalf the *main thing*—the central motivation for your life and faith.

———. *Humility—True Greatness*, Colorado Springs, CO: Multnomah Publishers.

Mahanaey paints a striking picture of the daily battle quietly raging within every Christian and asks whether you will passively accommodate the enemy of your soul—pride, or actively cultivate your best friend—humility. When you acknowledge the deception of pride and intentionally humble yourself, you become free to savor abundant mercies, unlikely graces, and a God glorifying life you won't want to miss.

Peace, Martha. *Attitudes of a Transformed Heart*, Bemidji, Minnesota: Focus Publishing, 2001.

Even Christians too often embrace a low view of God and, consequently, a casual view of sin and Scripture. This mindset bleeds through in the hidden attitudes of the heart.

This book is about being *"transformed by the renewing of your minds"* and not being conformed to the world's thinking (Ro 12:2). If you have a teachable heart, this book will expose wrong assumptions in the penetrating light of God's Word.

Pink, Arthur W. *The Attributes of God*, Grand Rapids, MI: Baker Book House, 1975.

Failure to understand God's character leads to a skewed perception of the Divine—one that is too often cast in our own image. Seeking to remedy this, Pink outlines seventeen key characteristics of the Almighty. Whether for our own spiritual growth or for ministering to counselees, it is imperative that we have a right view of God. Though a small book, it takes us into the presence of God and helps us to realize that we live before the God of Scripture.

Piper, John. *Desiring God,* Colorado Springs, CO: Multnomah Books, 1986.
A rich classic, Piper leads us into a healthy biblical study on Christian motivation. The communion of a longing soul and a satisfying Christ is at the center of God's plan. Join him as he unveils stunning, life-impacting truths you may have seen in the Bible but never dared to believe.

—-. *The Pleasures of God,* Colorado Springs, CO: Multnomah Publishers, 2000.
This is a book that simply brings forth the teaching *"It is all about God; He does things for His pleasure. Period."* Fully understanding the joy of God will draw the reader into an encounter with His overflowing, self-replenishing, all-encompassing grace—the source of living water that all Christians desire to drink. This book will again put God at the center of creation and leave the reader very satisfied in Him.

Sproul, R. C. *The Invisible Hand,* P & R Publishing, 1996.
The hand of providence is in all of life's experience. Here is a superb study in the style of Sproul that will encourage the reader to see God's sovereign purpose in all of life's "random" appearances.

Spurgeon, Charles H. *The Power of Prayer in the Believer's Life.* Lynnwood, Washington: Emerald Books, 1993. Internet accessed, June 25, 2013.
The title says it all from a prince among preachers. These

lessons on prayer should goad the combatant to the priority, privilege, and power of perseverant praying.

Tripp, Paul, and Tim Lane. *How People Change*, New Growth Press, second edition, May 22, 2008.

A changed heart is the bright promise of the Gospels. When the Bible talks about the gift of a new heart, it doesn't mean a heart that is immediately perfected, but a heart that is capable of being changed. Jesus' work on the cross targets our hearts—our core desires and motivations—and when our hearts change, our behavior changes. It is exciting to see the application of familiar Scripture portions come forth in a fresh, applicable way to help us keep a focus that honors God.

Vincent, Milton. *A Gospel Primer for Christians: Learning to See the Glories of God's Love*, The Lockman Foundation, 1960.

Milton learned the hard way that Christians also need the gospel every day to keep us from falling into a performance relationship with God. This book will help you experience the power of the Gospel more consistently. It is literally life changing.

Welch, Ed. *Addictions: A Banquet in the Grave*, Phillipsburg, NJ: P & R Publishing, 2001.

A worship disorder—this is how Edward T. Welch views addictions. *"Will we worship ourselves and our own desires,"* he writes, *"or will we worship the true God?"* Through these lens, the author discovers far more in Scripture on addictions than passages on drunkenness. There we learn the addict's true condition: it is like that of a guest at a banquet thrown by the woman, Folly; he is already in the grave (Prov. 9:13–18). Can we not escape our addictions? If we're willing to follow Jesus, the author says we have *"...immense hope: hope in God's forgiving grace, hope in God's love that is faithful even when we are not, and hope that God can give power so that we are no longer mastered by the addiction."* Each chapter concludes with "Practical Theology Guidance," as "You Face Your Own Addictions," and "As You Help Someone Else."

———. *Blame It on the Brain*, Phillipsburg, NJ: P & R Publishing, 1998. Dr. Welch views various "brain problems" through the lens of Scripture in this wonderful book. Ed distinguishes genuine brain disorders from problems rooted in the heart. Understanding the distinction will enable pastors, counselors, families, and friends to help others, or themselves deal with personal struggles. While focusing on a few common disorders, Ed lays out a series of practical steps adaptable to a wide range of conditions, habits, and addictions.

———. *When People Are Big and God Is Small*, Phillipsburg, NJ: P & R Publishing, 1997.
This excellent work deals with the idea that people are so desirous of pleasing men that they fail to walk in the fear of God. It is a very introspective book and one that calls for an honest inventory of heart motivations.

Websites for obtaining much of the materials mentioned above and other excellent resources:
Biblical Counseling Foundation:
<bcfministries.org>

Christian Counseling and Educational Foundation:
<ccef.org>

Cumberland Valley Bible Book Service:
<cvbbs.com>

National Association of Nouthetic Counselors:
<nanc.org>

Faith Baptist Church Counseling Ministries:
<fbclayfette.org>

Christian Book Distributors:
<christianbook.com>

Biblical Counseling Strengthening Ministries:
<mackministries.org>

Biblical Counseling Manual:
<ecoin.net/bcbook>

Timeless Texts:
<timelesstexts.com>

Women Helping Women Ministries:
<elysefitzpatrick.com>

Pure Life Ministries:
<purelifeministries.org>

Ministries for Children:<truthquest.net/aboutushome.html>

About the Author

Pastor Mark L. Graham has served the local church for nearly forty years. He has written extensively to provide biblical helps for those under his pastoral and counseling care. Founder of the Genesis Ministries, Inc., adjunct professor of biblical counseling for eight years with the Empire State Baptist Theological Seminary, Dr. Graham holds various degrees and diplomas in ministry, counseling and law. Currently, Pastor Graham resides with his wife, Diane, in Cazenovia, NY where he mines the riches of God's Word daily and shepherds the Grace Bible Church in nearby Fayetteville. The Grahams have four married children who serve Christ through the local church. They also enjoy their heritage of eleven delightful grandchildren, one of whom lives at home with Jesus.

CPSIA information can be obtained at www.ICGtesting.com
Printed in the USA
BVOW07s0007201113

336779BV00002B/6/P

9 781462 732180